The
Quinoa
Chronicles

The
Quinoa
Chronicles

A MEMOIR

How a humble food from the
High Andes became a worldwide sensation

STEPHEN L. GORAD

Stephen L. Gorad
New York

Published by:
Stephen L. Gorad
sgorad@gmail.com
www.quinoachronicles.com

Cover design by: Lynda Rae
Cover photo: *Salar de Uyuni*, Altiplano, Bolivia
© Vadim Petrakov/Shutterstock
Interior design by: Lynda Rae

First print edition published 2017
ISBN: 978-1975750459

This book is dedicated to
Paz y Amor

CONTENTS

FOREWORD

I WANTED TO LEARN TO MEDITATE. After five years as a chiropractor tending to the back pain of high-powered executives, I was fraying around the edges. Well, not exactly fraying, more like coming apart.

Visions of trekking through the snowy Himalayas to sit cross-legged before an Exotic Prince of Silence occupied my imagination, like an escape route. Ah! Silence. Quietude. Stillness.

I had no desire to attend a meditation class, read a spiritual book, or watch a self-help video. I wanted the real deal.

One day, an unusual looking patient appeared in my waiting room. Unusual because he didn't look at all like a stressed out executive. Dr. Stephen Gorad was more a hippy type; tall, with long reddish hair pulled into a ponytail, wire-rimmed glasses, old jeans, a green plaid flannel shirt, and the strangest shoes I'd ever seen. They looked like Chinese house slippers; black, and worn with no socks even though it was cold outside.

Steve had been in a car accident in Chile; a high impact head-on collision with a bus. The car was demolished, but miraculously he suffered no injuries except a twisted back.

Steve had spent lots of time in South America. In fact, I discovered that my new patient was responsible for bringing quinoa from its native country, Bolivia, to the States.

This was the early nineties and almost nobody had heard of quinoa, but I had. A nutritionist had recommended I add this protein rich grain to my diet since I was pretty much a vegetarian.

As Steve stood in his patient gown, I measured this, calculated that, and muscle-tested the appropriate joints. I wanted to tell him that the sandalwood oil he was wearing was a little strong, but as usual I kept this kind of opinion to myself.

I had Steve lie face down on the treatment table and put my hands on his back.

Silence. Quietude. Stillness.

I had put my hands on hundreds of people and usually, what I felt was …

Tension. Anxiety. Noise.

As I balanced the reflex points that ran up and down Steve's spine, I became strangely relaxed.

After I worked on him, instead of the usual explanation of what his treatment plan would be, I asked him,

"Do you meditate?"

"Yes," he said.

"Great. I want you to teach me."

Steve hesitated. He wasn't jumping at the idea. I liked that. He took his practice seriously.

"Look," I said, "I never ask anything of my patients. I just know this is the right thing. So, please, can't you just teach me?"

We agreed I would leave an hour after his next appointment. I was psyched!

Steve returned three days later and, again, I felt relaxed while working on him.

After his treatment, we went into the waiting room and sat cross-legged on the floor. I closed my eyes and followed his instructions, which involved my third eye and looking at the inner light. Energy began fluttering around my spine like a butterfly. After about a half an hour, he told me to open my eyes.

Silence. Quietude. Stillness.

Every time he came to the office, after his treatment we would meditate. My angst subsided, his back pain disappeared, and we became friends.

Steve meditated three to four hours a day. I was sure I would never be able to do that. I didn't even want to. It seemed absurd, indulgent and impractical. In spite of myself, I would go to Steve's apartment to meditate with him, or at least try to. Steve would sit tall, still and relaxed for hours on end, while I squirmed around, each minute seemingly endless. Little by little, I was able to be still and meditate without dying to get up, or incessantly looking at the clock, or even being aware of my surroundings.

Pretty soon, I discovered how much Steve loved food and cooking. He would prepare exotic quinoa dishes, like fried quinoa balls that resembled falafel, vegetarian quinoa "chicken" salad, quinoa pancakes, even amazingly delicious chocolate quinoa cake. Some of his other delicacies were his homemade, thick crust pizza, Vietnamese spring rolls, and his chocolate coconut walnut ecstasy squares.

Steve also became good friends with my husband, and we would all go to the country for meditation retreats.

Silence. Stillness. Quietude. Quinoa. Pizza. Trees. Sky. More Stillness.

I was with Steve on Christmas Eve 1992 when he got a letter from Tibet informing him they had succeeded in growing quinoa on their high plains. A professor at an agricultural school in Tibet was asking him to come and help them because, although they were growing it, they knew almost nothing about the sacred grain. He went. That was Steve. He was always ready to help, expecting nothing in return.

Like the time my drug-addicted brother Billy was stranded in Venezuela. Steve got on a plane and rescued him. In my book, *The Afterlife of Billy Fingers*, I tell the tale of that adventure. In the book Steve is called Guru Guy, a nickname Billy gave him.

In bringing quinoa to the United States and beyond, Steve has provided a unique and valuable service to our health, well-being and culture. The unlikely and fortuitous events that enabled him to do so are recounted in the pages that follow. It is a story only Steve could tell.

Annie Kagan

ACKNOWLEDGMENTS

THIS BOOK HAS BEEN OVER a decade in the making. The seed for it was planted when Jamie Matusow interviewed me for an article she was hoping to write on the origins of quinoa. That was in April of 2007. I'd known Jamie for many years, since the time she came to me with an idea for a quinoa recipe book. Jamie asked me how I first got involved with quinoa, and I answered by speaking non-stop for over four hours.

Jamie was thoroughly overwhelmed by my talk, and I was surprised by the sheer intensity of the stories that poured out of me. Somehow, in the heat of the moment she neglected to record the session, nor did she take notes. No article was forthcoming. But Jamie's interview showed me something very important; that I had a lot of unusual quinoa stories inside me waiting to be told. If only they could be coaxed out, and put securely on paper.

I decided to repeat the interview, with another interviewer and a voice recorder. I knew that in order for me to speak as I did the interviewer had to be sincerely interested. I asked a dear friend, Charlotte Richardson. We met over a three-day period in July 2008 and recorded hours of good story material. Unfortunately, due to a malfunction in the voice recorder, the recordings proved worthless. But much to my delight, Charlotte had taken copious handwritten notes on everything I said.

Those notes were the first words on paper, and they eventually became this book.

In the years that followed, Charlotte helped throughout the whole process of producing this book, including doing some major editing, and providing needed moral support. Thank you, Charlotte.

Others who kindly read and commented on earlier versions were William Owen Wallace, Erin McDonald, Karen Osborne, Andrew Mandel, Richard McGowen, Annie Kagan, Steven Mallis, and Elly Graham. Thank you.

Annie Kagan did much more than just read, comment, and edit early drafts of this book. She patiently guided me through the whole writing process. Annie has a wonderful book in publication, *The Afterlife of Billy Fingers*, so her guidance has been especially important for me. Thank you, Annie.

Lynda Rae, a dear friend and spiritual sister, was there near the beginning of my adventures with quinoa, and she is once again here, helping me finish this book and finally put it out to the public. Thank you, Lynda.

I'd like to also thank the people not mentioned in the book who worked at or supported the activities of Quinoa Corporation in the 1980s. You made this all possible: Crystal, Jules, Margaret, Denise, Garrett, Ann, Eugene, Ken, Berkeley, Patty, Gloria, Corbett, Donna, Jena, George, Jerry, Kim, Joanne.

And thank you to all the other friends and loves who kept me sane throughout these years—Anna Kiersnowska, Steve Wander, Marta Huepe, Mark Josephson, Gisela Smutny, Elena Eydelnant, Hsu Shih-Ling, Alejandro Celis, Gonzalo Perez, Mary Bruner, Don Seckler, Diane Lynn.

In Memoriam
Paz Maria Teresa Huneeus Martinez
September 23, 1944 - October 24, 2016

Colombia

Ecuador

* Quito

Peru

Brazil

Barranca

Lima

Cusco

Bolivia

Puno

Lago Titicaca

La Paz

Tiahuanaco

Altiplano

* Santa Cruz

Pacific Ocean

Arica

Isluga

Atacama Desert

Iquique

Salar de Uyuni

Paraguay

Antofagasta

Argentina

La Serena

* Totoral

Chile

Santiago

Linares
Concepcion

*

500 miles

"... the greatest service which can be rendered any country is to add an useful plant to its culture; especially a bread grain."

— Thomas Jefferson

CHAPTER ONE

Beginnings

IT WAS IN THE KITCHEN of a friend's apartment on the outskirts of Santiago, Chile that I fell deeply, madly, hopelessly in love with quinoa. The year was 1977 and I was on the last leg of a three-month trip to South America.

I put raw quinoa in a small pot, added twice the volume of water, and turned up the heat. I left the pot uncovered so I could watch it. I had no idea how to cook quinoa, as neither I, nor anyone I knew, had ever done so before. I just thought I'd prepare it like brown rice. The water boiled, the quinoa cooked, and my fate was sealed.

That moment would never have occurred if it weren't for a chain of serendipitous events.

It all began several years earlier with Oscar Ichazo, a most remarkable man, the founder and master of a mystical school called Arica. Oscar was the first person I'd ever heard speak the word "quinoa." He said it was an important food from his native country, Bolivia, and that it was a good thing to eat when doing spiritual practice. That was all I knew about it at the time.

STEPHEN L. GORAD

Oscar Ichazo

My history with Oscar's Arica School dates back to the winter of 1972. I was a clinical psychologist on staff at Boston State Hospital. I'd earned my Ph.D. the year before and was already Principal Psychologist of the Alcohol Unit. A colleague of mine left an Arica brochure on my desk announcing the arrival of a new method for consciousness development.

I'd been reading *In Search of the Miraculous* by P. D. Ouspensky, a book about the spiritual teachings of G. I. Gurdjieff. The brochure led me to believe that Oscar might be a living teacher like what Gurdjieff once was, someone who could show me what "real" life is about. Oscar's method promised to bring people to higher states of consciousness, and even enlightenment, through a series of highly programmed trainings. The core training of the School was called a 40 Day and one was to be held in Boston during the summer of 1973. I eagerly signed up for it.

When I told my boss at the hospital that I wanted to take forty days off from work, he told me, "Steve, if your mother died, I wouldn't give you two weeks off. The research you are doing is that important." I thought long and hard about what he said and realized I had to make a choice, a choice between two very different ways of life.

What my boss, a psychiatrist, actually meant was that it was important that I do the research and write the scientific papers that would have his name on them as first author. But I was the one who'd designed the study, and I did not think it was all that important. My choice was between staying with the status quo, a secure and probably lucrative career as a psychologist, or stepping out into the unknown in search of something, shall we say, more "miraculous."

Dr. Gorad at Boston State Hospital

I quit my position at the hospital and did the Arica 40 Day.

The first two people to show up for the training were Don McKinley and myself. The two of us talked as we waited for others to arrive. Don was clean cut, quiet, and with an understated temperament. Many people kidded him because he looked and sounded a lot like the actor, Henry Fonda. To me, having grown up in New York City, Don seemed like the sort of person who would be from someplace like Ohio; and in fact he was from Ohio, just like the other McKinley, the president. During the course of those forty days, Don and I formed a close friendship that would last for many years. Yet at the beginning, neither he nor I had any idea what was to come, and what quinoa had in store for us.

Don McKinley

The 40 Day training turned me completely around. Before, everything about my life had been meticulously conventional. I was smart, loved science, went to the prestigious Bronx High School of Science and afterward to M.I.T. I did my graduate work at Boston University and began a career as a clinical psychologist. I was doing well.

I'd bought a townhouse, a big house in the South End of Boston, and rented rooms out to young people, many of them hippies. They laughed at me because I was so straight, so uptight. They somehow lived free and easy lives, without jobs, without responsibil-

The author as an idealistic young man

ities. I was still going to work every day and I didn't do drugs.

When I joined the Arica School, everything changed. Don and other 40 Day graduates moved in, and at one point twenty of us lived together as a commune. I was no longer a psychologist. I had become an "Arican."

When the training ended, I had the thought, *I don't know what I'm going to do today, or the next day, or the day after that.* My life had always been obsessively ordered, every moment following the next according to schedule. After the 40 Day I found that days just naturally flowed into one another without any planning. Each and every day took care of itself, and my life has been like that ever since.

Doing an Arica meditation

In the years after the 40 Day, I did other Arica trainings as they were offered, and I also explored other spiritual teachings from various traditions, including Hinduism, Buddhism, Sufism, and mystic Christianity. I became a serious seeker of Truth, an experienced meditator, and even a healer of some skill and reputation.

I began to travel . . . a lot. As part of the Arica School, you could go just about anywhere in the world, have a place to stay, and be with like-minded people. For a while I lived in a VW camper and traveled around the United States, stopping wherever Aricans had formed small communities. I spent a winter meditating in Paris, traveled throughout Europe, and went alone to a Hindu Kumbha Mela festival in India. Through the early 70s, Don and I kept in close touch from wherever we were.

During those years, and as far back as I can remember, I had a fascination with food and cooking.

My mother told me that, when I was three, I wanted to cook with her. She told me, "You stood next to me in the kitchen and with your dirty little fingers made a small pie while I made mine." I was always interested in food, but not just any food. My interests lay in unusual foods. My father taught me not to follow ordinary recipes and to try new things. He put ketchup in his chicken soup, grape jelly on an omelet, and he showed me how to put butter inside a slice of toast. To this day, I do not know how to follow a recipe.

Later in life I experimented with all sorts of diets. The macrobiotic diet was an important one, but I also experimented with raw food diets, vegetarian and vegan diets, and all sorts of fasting. I tried just about everything, and for a while I ate only sprouted wheat berries.

In the summer of 1977 Don and I flew to Hawaii to hang out at a residential Arica 40 Day training on Maui for about a hundred new students. Lennie and Amy, dear friends who had lived in my commune in Boston, were in charge of the kitchen. They knew I was an excellent cook. I told them I wanted to help, but Lennie said an emphatic "No." He mumbled something about state regulations and that no one was permitted in the kitchen without a TB test. Toward the end of the training he inexplicably changed his mind. He had one dinner open in his agenda and asked me if I wanted to prepare a meal. I happily said I would and then proceeded to create a six-course, natural food Chinese banquet.

Several students at the training asked if they could help, something that had never happened before. I welcomed them and gave each the task of chopping this or stirring that. Huge bowls of vegetables, brown rice, tofu, and other exotic ingredients were magically transformed into many beautiful, sizzlingly delicious dishes. There was a blur of frantic activity, and I felt as if I was conducting an orchestra playing Stravinsky's *Le Sacre du Printemps*. The kitchen lit up with wild and wonderful energy.

When the food was cooked and ready, we served it in the dining room one course at a time, and each dish was greeted by the waiting group first with surprise, then amazement, and then ecstatic joy. They couldn't believe how great the food was and neither could I. At one point people got up to leave, not realizing that there were several more courses to come.

When the meal was over, people in the dining room were shouting for me to show myself. Some students came into the kitchen, grabbed me, lifted me off my feet, and carried me into the dining room. About a hundred people were standing, some on chairs, cheering loudly and applauding. I was quite over-whelmed by the whole scene and very happy indeed.

Sometimes energy flows into an event in unexpected ways and creates something extraordinary, and that something then has totally unexpected consequences.

In the back of the room was a Chilean woman, tears running down her face. She came up to me and told me she had never tasted such a delicious meal in all her life. She owned a restaurant in Chile and asked me to go and take charge of it.

I'd never been anywhere in South America, as I never before had any reason or even desire to go. My response to most every-thing during those years was to say "yes." Whether a proposed plan actually happened or not came somehow out of the partic-ular circumstances of the moment. Sometimes things happened and sometimes they didn't, but I never wanted to stand in the way. So I said I would go to Chile, but I had absolutely no idea how I'd get there.

Much to my delight, the Chilean woman's daughter, Cristina, came to me a few days later and offered me a free, round-trip air ticket to Chile. She wanted me to accompany her, to help ease her transition home after

Cristina Terre

experiencing such high energy at the training.

I now had both an exciting job in Chile and the means to get there. I was in heaven. An amazing new adventure had just materialized for me out of thin air.

Don McKinley and other friends didn't want me to go. Chile was under the Pinochet dictatorship at the time, and they thought it could be dangerous. I didn't care. I had no idea what I was getting into, but I had a free ticket and a restaurant to run, so I was going. Don stayed in Hawaii.

Since Chile is in the southern hemisphere the seasons are the reverse of ours. When I arrived in Santiago with Cristina it was early spring. The trees were budding, a few flowers were out, the days were warming slowly, and people's energies were just beginning to stir. I spent a couple of days getting adjusted, and then I asked Cristina to take me to the restaurant. She went to inquire about it, and discovered that her mother didn't actually own the restaurant. It was a city government concession in a public park, and while her mother was out of the country, someone else was given the rights to operate it.

What?!!!

I'd traveled all that way to Chile to manage a restaurant only to learn that it was not going to happen. At first I was upset and more than a little disoriented.

I'm in Chile, damn it, on the other side of the world. What do I do now?

But then I settled myself down and had a good laugh. This sort of thing wasn't new to me. Many times I'd walk into a certain situation, and though I was there to do one thing, the actual reason I was there turned out to be something totally different.

Relax, Steve . . . everything is fine . . . just go with the flow.

Thus began my adventures in South America—new places, new people, and new experiences. I spent the first month in Chile, mostly around Santiago, mostly meeting the bright and beautiful people there who had been following Oscar Ichazo's teachings.

Cristina and I then loaded up her Chevy convertible and drove for several days up the coast, through exotic places with strange names—La Serena, Antofagasta, Iquique, and the Atacama Desert, known as the "deadest desert in the world." At last we arrived in Arica, the charming seaside town near the Peruvian border where Oscar first trained students from the U.S. and for which his mystical School is named.

We spent the night in Arica and then flew the short distance to La Paz in Bolivia, simply for an adventure. La Paz is built into a great bowl-shaped depression in the Altiplano, the vast high plain of Bolivia, and is some 12,000 feet above sea level, where the air is thin and cold, and the sun burning hot. We looked around the city for several days, explored the nearby archeological ruins at Tiahuanaco, the Valley of the Moon, with its alien-looking rock formations, and Lago Titicaca, the highest lake in the world, with perhaps

La Paz, Bolivia

the funniest name. We then met up with some other Chileans living in La Paz. One of them was married to Oscar's sister, Maggi, so we ended up spending a lot of time in the Ichazo family home. I met Oscar's father, Don Antenor, an important Bolivian General, and visited the Ichazos' remote silver mine, built originally by Spanish conquistadors.

The ruins at Tiahuanaco

Bolivia was, and is still, a very poor country. I'd seen people living in poverty before during my trip to India, but Bolivia was different. It was dirt poor, but oddly quiet and peaceful. India, in contrast, was chaotic, colorful and loud.

I saw many strange things in Bolivia, and I also found myself doing some strange things. I took the psychedelic drug LSD twice, once at the Tiahuanaco ruins and once at the Ichazo mine. Under the influence of LSD, I felt the depth and strength of my connection to both the land and the people of the Andes Mountains. It was as if I'd been there before, perhaps in past lives. It was a surprising discovery.

Coca leaf could be found everywhere in Bolivia. The hotels all served coca leaf tea and told visitors that it would help with the headaches and fatigue that come with altitude sickness. The tea didn't actually work, but chewing coca leaves did help. I also had my first experience with cocaine. The cocaine was 100% pure, and people snorted fat lines of it through plastic pen barrels. It made me wonder how people in the States ever got anything from the highly cut, tiny quantities of drug they were using.

I love marketplaces, love seeing the people and everything they have to sell, particularly the food. No matter where I might be traveling, I ask to go to the food markets, and even the super-markets if there are any. In a La Paz street market, I saw Aymara women with their characteristic bowler hats and long puffy skirts, sitting on the ground, barefoot, with sacks of foodstuffs to sell.

They were surrounded by all kinds and shapes of potatoes—*chuño* (freeze dried potato), *oca* (Oxalis tuberosa), *ulluco* (Ullucus tuberosus); dried multi-colored corn—both loose and on the cob, and also puffed, some with gigan-tic kernels; many different kinds of spices; the ubiqui-tous coca leaf . . . and then I saw a big open sack of something else.

La Paz street market

It looked sort of like a grain, but small and whitish in color. At first I thought it might be a type of millet, but it was flat instead of round, and not so yellow. It was shaped like a hockey puck, but miniscule. It didn't look at all like a bean, a spice, or anything that I'd ever seen before. I walked over, dipped my hand in, and ran some through my fingers.

I asked the woman sitting silently nearby, *"Oye Mamita. ¿Qué es esto?"* She answered, *"quinua."* Aha! *This is quinoa, that food Oscar told us about.* I bought a kilo from the woman, and stored it away, deep inside my backpack.

In the late 60s I'd studied and experimented with the macrobiotic diet. It was both a diet and a life philosophy, developed by George Ohsawa from Japan, that emphasized grains; so I already knew a lot about grains, but absolutely nothing about quinoa. Grains had been my staple food for years, and I tried every

Close-up of quinoa grain

one I could find. I was off the strict macrobiotic diet by this time, but I still loved eating and learning about grains. Finding one that I'd never eaten before was a big deal for me.

After our month of adventures in Bolivia, Cristina and I took the slow train down from La Paz to Arica, passing through some extraordinary, other-worldly scenery. At one point we saw flocks of bright pink flamingos happily living in the midst of a completely barren mountain landscape, something I never could have imagined. It was a great relief to be at sea level once again, as breathing in the oxygen-poor air of La Paz had been difficult. We recovered her car and made the long drive back to Santiago, ending our journey at the apartment of Pilar Valdes, one of Oscar's Chilean community of followers.

So there I was in Pilar's kitchen, cooking quinoa (See Recipe, pg. 193) for the first time, the quinoa I had bought in La Paz.

Quinoa is different from all other grains in one very unique and specific way. With all other grains, the germ (or embryo) is embedded in the body of the seed (inside the endosperm), but with quinoa, the germ wraps around the outside of the seed. When you cook quinoa the germ swells, sometimes unwrapping and forming little

Quinoa showing germ

hooks and curls that are quite visible. As the quinoa cooked, hundreds of these tiny little squiggles unfolded in the pot. I'd never seen anything quite like it.

The individual raw quinoa grains were an opaque white, but as they cooked they slowly became translucent. This change

Partially cooked quinoa showing white eyes

occurred from the outside in toward the center, so at one point the grains looked like little white eyes. I was totally fascinated by what I saw, the newness and the beauty of it all. Fifteen short minutes later, the eyes disappeared, the grains were totally translucent, and I understood that the quinoa was thoroughly cooked.

I then ate some, and in those moments a curious thought occurred to me.

Was this why I had come all the way to South America — to discover quinoa?

Like all grains, quinoa is quite bland. It doesn't have the taste appeal of a ripe mango, dark chocolate, a fine wine, or French cheese. Taste-wise, one could say it is rather boring. Yes, it has a distinct, but subtle, sort of earthy flavor that can distinguish it from other grains, but that is not what made quinoa so special to me. What was special was the effect it had on my body. It was as if my body was shouting, *Yes, yes, yes . . . this is good. I want it!*

This was not a mental judgment or opinion. It was something much deeper than that. It doesn't matter whether you like the taste of quinoa or not. It doesn't matter whether you know anything about it or not. It doesn't matter why you are eating it.

If you eat it, quinoa will do its magic in your body.

If you are conscious in your body, if you are sensitive enough, you can tell when something is truly nourishing you, and your body knows that quinoa is doing just that. Your mind can tell you all sorts of interesting things about food, but your body knows what it wants.

I have never ever eaten quinoa and then been sorry, and I can't say that about many other foods.

What Is Quinoa?

Standing in Pilar's kitchen, all I knew was that I was fascinated with this strange little grain, and that Oscar had said it was important. I didn't know anything else about it, but I wanted to. I thought there must be information somewhere, so

I asked my new friends in Chile to help me find out more.

A beautiful young woman named Paz Huneeus got me what I sought, and that wasn't all she did. Springtime was in all its splendor in Chile by the time Cristina and I got back from Bolivia. Flowers were blooming everywhere, and the streets of Santiago were heavy with sweet smells. I could feel the energy of new life moving through my body, and my heart was opening

Paz Huneeus

wide to all the beauty around me. There was a certain magic in the air. There was Paz! As it turned out, quinoa wasn't the only thing I fell in love with during my trip to South America. Paz quickly became the love of my life, and later, my wife.

Paz was the type of person who got things done. She found me an obscure scientific article by Professor Ingo Junge called "Lupine and Quinoa Research and Development in Chile." It was precisely what I needed. Junge's paper surprised me with all sorts of useful information.

There was nothing at all ordinary about quinoa.

What jumped out at me was how radically different quinoa was from all the other grains from a nutritional perspective.

His study of the quinoa grain revealed many outstanding properties, chief among these being its high protein content. All grains have some protein. Rice has about 7.5%. Some varieties of wheat have as much as 14%, but quinoa tops them all. It has between 11% and 21.3% depending on the variety, with an average of 16.2%, significantly higher than that of any other grain.

Of equal and perhaps greater importance than the quantity of protein is the quality of quinoa protein.

All of the essential amino acids, i.e., those that the human body cannot manufacture itself, and thus must be introduced in the diet, are represented. In quinoa they account for 37% of the total protein content. Moreover, the relative proportions of these amino acids, which determine their usefulness to the human body, are closer to the ideal pattern (as set by the United Nations Food and Agriculture Organization) than any other food from the vegetable kingdom.

This makes the quality of quinoa protein roughly equivalent to that of milk (casein) or egg (albumin), without any of the disadvantages of coming from an animal source.

I found out that quinoa protein is high in both lysine and the sulfur bearing amino acids (methionine and cysteine), making it a more perfect protein than that from other grains or legumes. Most grains are low in lysine, and most legumes, including soybeans, are low in the sulfur bearing amino acids.

A lot of the nutritional value of quinoa is packed inside the germ, that little white curl that detaches from quinoa when you cook it. It is unusually large, accounting for 25% of the entire seed by weight, and contains 48.5% protein and 28% oil.

Aside from its excellent quality protein, quinoa provides a rich and balanced source of other vital nutrients, including starch, sugars, oil (over 50% of which is the essential linoleic acid), fiber, minerals like calcium, potassium, and iron, and vitamins, particularly B complex and E.

The information I had from Junge's paper was leagues beyond the few facts that originally interested me in quinoa. I could see from a scientific perspective perhaps why my body responded so positively to it.

To me, quinoa seemed almost miraculous.

Paz also put me in touch with a doctor at a Santiago hospital, Mario Gonzales. He told me that new mothers who can't produce enough breast milk hire wet nurses to provide milk for their babies. He said that Mapuche (the sea level-dwelling indigenous people of Chile) women serving as wet nurses produced far more than the normal woman's supply of breast milk, and that they all ate quinoa on a regular basis. His striking conclusion was that women who eat quinoa are better able to produce breast milk.

Dr. Gonzales suggested that I go visit his brother Emilio, a farmer in the Linares region, some two hundred miles south of Santiago. Emilio Gonzales used to head a quinoa growing project in Chile under the auspices of the Allende government. His project involved sea level quinoa, a small, dark, bitter variety, very different from the type now imported to the United States from Bolivia or Peru. The Allende government recognized that quinoa is a remarkably high quality food and that its production and use should be promoted to improve the diet and health of the Chilean people. Then, when the Pinochet regime took over Chile in the 1973 coup, all quinoa-related work was halted by order of the new government.

Paz and I visited Emilio. He was absolutely delighted that a "gringo" was interested enough in quinoa to come visit him at his farm. I finally got to meet and talk with a real quinoa expert, and I learned a lot from him. Quinoa is an amazing food crop, but it also has a problem; the grains have a bitter, resin-type coating, called saponin, that has to be removed before the grain is edible. Saponins are naturally occurring glycoside chemicals that produce foam when mixed in water, much like soap.

Paz and I also went to see Ingo Junge, the professor at the University of Concepción, whose paper I had read and who claimed to have developed machinery and a process for removing the saponin. Professor Junge proudly took us to see his invention, which was set up in a building by the side of his house. What we saw put us in shock. The machinery looked like it was rigged together by a madman, or a Gyro Gearloose. It was simply a washing machine and a dryer, with tiny little cups moving on wires to carry the quinoa from one processing step to another. That was his so-called industrial process.

I couldn't believe that the man I so admired as *the* expert on quinoa had invented such a crazy contraption. The problem of saponin removal would need a better solution than this if what I found myself thinking were to actually happen. I was already beginning to see quinoa as a food for everyone.

Having thoroughly informed myself about the remarkable nutritional characteristics of quinoa, I then asked myself, *What kind of plant produces such an amazing food?* I knew about the grain, the seed, but I knew nothing about the quinoa plant. I'd visited Emilio Gonzales' sea level farm in Chile, but I soon came to understand that quinoa was grown all throughout the Andean region, in the mountains and high altitude valleys of Colombia, Ecuador, Argentina and Peru, and up on the high plains of Bolivia, Peru and Chile. The real heart of quinoa production and use seemed to be Bolivia, so I turned my investigations back in that direction.

The Bolivian Altiplano

When one looks out at the Altiplano, the high plains of the Andes mountains of Bolivia, with an altitude of 12,500 feet or higher, all you can see are vast expanses of flat barren earth, bordered in the far distance by massive mountain peaks, some volcanic, some snowcapped. There is not a tree in sight, nor any other sign of plant life except for small clumps of needle-pointed grass and some scraggly brush. Dust and dirt are everywhere, at times much of it hanging in the wind. The sun is hot, with an overpowering presence, but enter the shade and you feel immediately just how cold the air is.

This, I was told, was the legendary birthplace of quinoa.

What kind of plant grows in a region as barren and forbidding as the Altiplano? The Andes is not a place for the delicate or frail, neither in plants or animals, nor in man. High altitudes produce conditions of unusual environmental stress, including cold, high winds, extreme differences in daytime and nighttime

The Bolivian Altiplano

temperatures, low humidity, atmospheric pressure reductions of almost 50%, and high levels of solar and cosmic radiation.

The plants that we are accustomed to seeing at sea level do not exist on the Altiplano. Cattle do not do well there. Internal combustion engines falter easily in the oxygen-poor atmosphere. Fires are hard to light and even more difficult to maintain. The soil of the Altiplano is poor and sandy and in some areas highly alkaline. In some parts rainfall doesn't exist, and when it does, it averages less than four inches annually.

I found it incredible that the quinoa plant can grow under these conditions. Not only does it grow, it grows well. It grows in the poorest of soils. It tolerates the highly alkaline land surrounding the Andean salt flats, the *Salar de Uyuni*. It endures periodic frosts, in some areas on a monthly basis, as well as the severest of droughts. I was told that if you deprive a young quinoa plant of water, it will not grow more than a few inches tall, but it will still mature and produce seed. Such is the vitality of this plant.

Once again, I had the sense that there was something miraculous about quinoa—quinoa as a food, but also quinoa as a plant.

This plant was discovered and put to good use long ago by the indigenous populations of the Andean mountains. We know that it has been used for over three, and possibly as many as seven, thousand years by mountain-dwelling peoples. Quinoa seed found at archeological sites attests to its use in antiquity.

The Inca civilization, which dates back to about 1200 A.D., promoted the use and cultivation of quinoa throughout their vast Andean Kingdom, stretching from Chile in the south to Colombia in the north. Quinoa shared its place with corn, which was grown at lower elevations, and potatoes as the staple foods for the Empire. The Inca considered quinoa a sacred plant.

Following Francisco Pizarro's conquest of the Inca territories beginning in 1532, the cultivation and use of quinoa was largely disrupted, but not entirely halted. The new Spanish landlords introduced wheat and livestock to the fertile valleys and lowlands and embraced corn and potatoes, exporting them back to Europe.

Quinoa went underground and remained almost exclusively a food for poor, rural native peoples. Even in the last century, in the larger cities of the Andean countries, quinoa was thought of as poor people's food, hardly fit for human consumption. Even so, there were over ten million Aymara and Quechua speaking people of indigenous descent relying upon quinoa as their primary source of nourishment.

The indigenous peoples of ancient times made use of the entire quinoa plant. The seed or grain was generally ground, either raw or toasted, into flour and baked into bread or biscuits (See Recipes, pg. 194). The whole grain was used for making porridges (See Recipe, pg. 195) and soups (See Recipe, pg. 196), or as a mash for making an alcoholic beverage called *chicha* (See Recipe, pg. 197). The green leaves were eaten raw in salads or cooked as a vegetable, somewhat like spinach (See Recipe, pg. 198).

Even the bitter tasting, soapy saponin resin, washed off prior to cooking, was used by native women as a shampoo and hair conditioner. The long woody stalks were burned as fuel, and the alkaline ash from the burned stalk was moistened and pressed into small cakes called *lliptu*. This was traditionally chewed along with coca leaves to activate and release coca's potent medicinal substances.

Because of its many uses, it has been said that quinoa was to the indigenous peoples of the Andes what the buffalo was to the Indians of the North American plains.

Quinoa grain was not only used as a food. It was also considered a folk medicine, used internally as well as externally in the form of poultices. It was said to cure anything from bruises to bad temper. Different varieties of quinoa were used for their effect on different body functions. One variety called *Quinua Ccoito* was even said to enhance sexual performance. All of these uses of quinoa continue until this day among the indigenous Andean peoples.

Considering the fact that the Chilean researchers found quinoa important for producing breast milk, and its vital functions in the lives of Andean natives, it is no wonder that quinoa is known as *la chisiya mama*, the all-providing mother grain.

I often think of quinoa as "milk of the earth."

When I began studying quinoa and then telling people about it, I was sometimes asked, "So why haven't we heard about this food before?" I wondered the same thing, and it troubled me. *Why was something as good as quinoa so totally unknown in my world? How could that be? Was there something I was missing?*

One assumes that things happen only when people make them happen. Is it possible that no one had yet thought seriously of doing anything with quinoa; or perhaps they thought of it, but didn't or couldn't do anything about it?

Surely someone somewhere had an encounter with quinoa before me, yet nothing much came of it. My meeting with quinoa, in contrast, was nothing short of a life-altering experience. It was as if an overwhelming force took hold of me and wouldn't let me go. I watched it cook and I was hooked. I ate it and I was doubly hooked. *How does something like this happen? Is it just an issue of timing, destiny, or what?*

The truth of the matter is that quinoa was not entirely unknown. People in the scientific community had been writing about it for many years.

In 1975 the National Academy of Sciences published the book *Underexploited Tropical Plants with Promising Economic Value*, in which quinoa was called "one of the best sources of protein in the vegetable kingdom."

Dr. Noel D. Vietmeyer, perhaps the world's most prominent spokesperson for unknown and underutilized food crops at the time, was the staff study director for that publication. His high praise of quinoa was extremely important for me, as he was known to be a reputable scientific authority in the United States. I often used his words to back up my bold, seemingly impossible, claims about quinoa. His recognition of quinoa's excellence meant that I wasn't totally crazy or alone in my fascination with the grain.

There had been several other earlier articles and scientific papers on quinoa in English and even more in Spanish. These articles went largely unnoticed by the public.

In a 1916 *National Geographic* article, "Staircase Farms of the Ancients," the author writes:

> "Two species of pigweed are regularly grown in the valleys that lead up to the Pass of La Raya, between Cuzco and Lake Titicaca. The largest species, which often attains a height of 3 or 4 feet, is called quinoa, while the small species, seldom more than a foot high and often only 5 or 6 inches, is called cañihua. In general appearance both species are much like our pigweed, but they are regularly planted and harvested by the Peruvians, and are in fact the only seed crops grown in the elevated districts that are too cold for maize."

The 1921 book, *The New Dietetics, What to Eat and How; A Guide to Scientific Feeding in Health and Disease,* by John Harvey Kellogg, of Kellogg cereal fame, states:

> "Quinoa, a cultivated pigweed, was a staple food of the natives of Mexico [sic] and South America before the conquest of these regions by Cortez [sic]. It is said to have produced prodigious crops. The seed is rich in protein, of which the flour contains 19 per cent, with 60 per cent of starch and 5 per cent of fat. . . . A Scotchman resident in Peru, where quinoa is still much used, declares it to be preferable to oatmeal as a breakfast food."

One of the important reasons that quinoa didn't make it into the public eye was the myth that quinoa cannot be grown outside of its Andean homeland. This myth developed out of several failed attempts to grow quinoa in North America and Europe.

In 1956 Elizabeth Eiselen's *Quinoa, a Potentially Important Food Crop of the Andes* stated:

> "In spite of numerous attempts, [quinoa] has never been successfully introduced elsewhere. When it has been tried at high elevations in the United States, the plant has flourished during the long summer days, reaching heights of seven feet, but the seed does not mature before the plants are killed by the winter cold."

Furthermore, it seems that no one believed that South American farms could ever supply the world markets. People assumed that Andean quinoa would never be produced on a scale large enough to succeed as an export crop.

I eventually learned that all these conclusions were erroneous.

It also troubled me greatly when I noticed that quinoa was not well thought of in its native lands. There was a widespread, totally misguided prejudice against it. South Americans of mixed or European blood considered it dirty, inedible, something fit only for chicken feed. It was food for indigenous peoples, for the poorest of the poor.

Nobody seemed to know about or appreciate quinoa's nutritional excellence. In the 1970s, throughout South America, you could not find quinoa in a restaurant or supermarket. If you wanted quinoa you had to grow it yourself or buy it at an indigenous street market. This situation is quite similar to the early prejudice against peanuts, once thought of as black slave food in the United States. Unfortunately, an anti-quinoa prejudice still exists in the generations of South Americans who were brought up with these beliefs.

Quinoa's lack of status led a prescient Peruvian researcher, who knew the true value of quinoa, to remark that "the shortest marketing route for quinoa from Cuzco (the former capital of the Inca Empire) to Lima (the modern capital of Peru) may be through the U.S. health food market." He hoped that marketing quinoa in the U.S. might enhance its appeal to South American consumers. It did.

CHAPTER TWO

Sitting in Limbo

MY TRIP TO SOUTH AMERICA included one month in Chile, a month in Bolivia, and then another month in Chile. When it was over, I flew back to the United States, but my heart was still in Chile. I was very much in love with Paz, and she with me, and now she was very far away on the southern side of the globe. I knew I would return to Chile, but first there were things I had to do back home. Of course I was thinking about quinoa.

While I was in Chile, Don McKinley had moved to Boulder, Colorado, and that is where I caught up with him. I told Don everything I'd learned about quinoa, about how truly amazing it is. I bombarded him with my enthusiasm. I couldn't stop myself. Don had been trained in advertising and marketing and immediately saw the potential for doing business with quinoa. "Steve, if this stuff is as good as you say it is, surely we could sell it." He got as excited as I was and wanted to move forward immediately with a plan.

I had Paz send a fifty-pound sack of quinoa to us in Boulder, perhaps the first shipment of quinoa to cross from South to

North America. She was able to do this easily, since at the time the Chilean government was trying to encourage exports; they even air freighted the sample for free.

As a first step, Don suggested that we see what people in the natural food industry in California would say. They would know if anyone would want it, and if we could make a business out of it. We hopped in Don's car and drove off to see Jimmy Silver at Erewhon Trading Company in Los Angeles, one of the leading natural food companies at the time. We showed him some quinoa. I talked glowingly about what it was, and then we gave him some to take home, to cook and taste. The next day Jimmy told us he liked it, that his whole family liked it. "If you bring it here, we'll sell it," he told us. We gave it to several other people to try, and everyone liked it and thought it was a great food with an interesting story.

But Don and I had no idea how we could import it. We had a wonderful product, but no business plan, no idea of what to do.

We never totally forgot about quinoa, but nothing more was to happen for quite a while.

During the next three years, between 1977 and 1980, I went back and forth to Chile to see Paz. At a certain point, I cleverly figured out that I could spend the spring and summer in the States, and since the seasons are the reverse in Chile, if I went down there during our fall, I could have an endless sequence of only springs and summers. My plan worked great for a while. The third year, circumstances switched me back the other way, falls and winters all year long. I learned the hard way that you cannot fool Mother Nature.

Don stayed in Boulder, worked in an advertising company, and then started his own business, Don McKinley Associates.

He and I also started a small business together, Lambsbread Woolens. We imported Pilar Valdes' hand loomed, naturally dyed woolen bedspreads and pillows from Chile and tried selling them in the U.S. Don created the business strategy and set up the marketing from Boulder, while I put up the money and handled supply from down in Chile. Pilar's woolen textiles were just gorgeous, but we could never get the sizing right. The artisanal wool she used shrank and expanded depending upon the humidity in the air.

That business failed, but it was the start of Don and me working together.

Don created a stable life for himself in Boulder. I traveled back and forth and gained familiarity with Chilean and South American culture.

My relationship with Paz continued growing. She had been a student of Oscar's during the earliest days of his teaching. At one point, I realized that many things had changed in the Arica School and that her ideas about Oscar were based largely on outdated memories. I thought she needed to come to New York City, where Oscar was living, to see him and get herself unstuck from the past. I also wanted to introduce her to other spiritual teachers of mine in the States, like Swami Muktananda. I invited her to come back with me, and called the trip the "Magical Mystery Tour."

We came to the States in the summer of 1979, and of course we visited Don in Boulder. Paz had a Chilean

Paz Huneeus

friend living there, Silvia Urrutia. She was married to an American, David Cusack, and we visited with them as well.

When I met David that first time I felt something about him that made me uncomfortable, although I couldn't put my finger on it. I also sensed something about his relationship with Silvia that bothered me. The next time I saw him they were no longer together.

Silvia Urrutia, pregnant with Daniela, and David Cusack

David had a Ph.D. in political science, but his interests and work were in the international agricultural development field. He had founded a nonprofit, Sierra Blanca Associates, and had development projects in Colorado and in South America. One of David's projects was with Dr. Mario Tapia, an esteemed scientist at the International Potato Center in Peru who had a long history of working with quinoa.

I was happy to meet David since he seemed to be exactly the sort of person who would know about quinoa. I thought perhaps he could help Don and me do something with it. I brought the subject up, and David did indeed know about quinoa, but instead of helping, he tried to discourage me. He definitely wasn't interested in working with it himself, as he didn't think quinoa was at all important. He summed up his opinion with, "Quinoa's been tried several times before, with no success. Forget about it."

Paz stayed with me in the States for several months. From Boulder we went to San Francisco, Boston, and finally to New

York City. When we arrived in New York it was during the height of the disco craze. Disco music was playing everywhere. Young men with boomboxes blaring carried the heavy beat of disco into the streets. "Ain't no stopping us now …. we're on the move …. ain't no stopping us now …. we're in the groove." It was an exciting time to be in the City. Paz saw Oscar there, as I had hoped she would. I had my time with him, too, the three of us together in his apartment on the upper east side of Manhattan. It was an experience I will never forget.

I wish I could describe all that happened during our night with Oscar, or at least say something useful about what kind of person he is, but honestly, nothing I say will ever do complete justice to that event or to him.

Much to my surprise Oscar flattered me, praising my spiritual level and my capacity for love. But in other moments he scolded me without mercy. How does someone say the words "I despise you," yet at the same time communicate only love? He did that. We drank fine scotch and smoked well into the early morning hours, and the energy never went down, only up. It got so high at times that I was sure I would pass out, but I didn't. At one point I made and served tea to try and calm things down. It didn't work. My efforts were ignored. He hit me hard in the head several times. The blows were sudden, unexpected and fast, like bolts of lightning coming out of nowhere. Amazingly he didn't hurt me. To the contrary, he somehow cured all the nagging pains I'd had for months in my neck and shoulders. We conducted lengthy conversations in what sounded like Chinese and Japanese, two languages I do not know. Yet we understood each other perfectly. We spoke of love, and of God's will.

Oscar (as if in despair): "The world is in such a miserable state. Everyone is asleep."

Me: "But Oscar, we are in God's hands!"

Oscar: "Yes, but that is us!"

We laughed and cried together. All in all, it was the most intense single experience in my lifetime, and it changed me forever. Afterward, for about six months, I could barely tolerate being with "normal" people, unless I had several drinks under my belt. Oscar was so real that everyone else seemed disappointingly fake. And during that same period, my personal energy was such that more women were attracted to me than ever before or after. Thank you, Oscar!

Paz went back home to Chile, and I realized it was time for me to move there as well. In 1980 we had a civil wedding ceremony before some sort of government official. I'll never forget taking our marriage vows, in Spanish, beneath a large photo of General Augusto Pinochet. The dour woman that married us had no sense of humor whatsoever and spoke only of sin and the grim responsibilities of marriage. She went on and on about rules and regulations. Paz and I found the whole thing very funny.

We rented a small, totally empty apartment in the Providencia section of

Paz and I get married

Santiago that didn't even have a refrigerator when we moved in. We had no money, no furniture, and no possessions, but we were happy.

Life was sweet in Santiago

I did massage and healing work, taught classes in meditation, bodywork, health, and cooking, and I wrote for *Clan Familiar*, a Chilean women's magazine. The articles I wrote covered a wide range of topics, including how to make sprouts, how to grow an avocado tree as an indoor plant, how to do foot reflexology, cooking in the New Age, the power of breath, and various topics concerning meditation. I wrote in English and had the pieces translated into Spanish. I also formulated, manufactured, and sold the first granola to ever appear in Chile.

Life was sweet for about two years.

Let's Grow Quinoa

In 1981, I got a letter from Don asking me for some quinoa. I bought a kilo in the market and mailed it off to him.

Months later, I found out why Don had asked me to send him quinoa. Don had what he described as an epiphany, an experience of "direct voice contact from spiritual guides." He said it felt like a lightning bolt had made him see with perfect clarity that the only sensible way to introduce quinoa into the United States was to grow it in Colorado. This epiphany, one of only two or three in his lifetime, was what finally cemented Don's resolve to actually do something with quinoa.

Much to my surprise, Don and another Arican, Peter Drake, met with David Cusack to talk about Don's idea. Peter knew David and introduced Don to him, and the two of them talked David into getting involved. This time, for some reason, David was completely receptive to working with quinoa.

The three of them picked a remote place in Colorado called the San Luis Valley for planting their first crop. David had good connections with farmers in the Valley, an economically depressed agricultural area in the Rocky Mountains where they grew potatoes as well as the barley for Coors beer. David's father had been a potato farmer in Colorado, so David knew who was doing what.

The Valley is actually a high altitude flat plain, sort of similar to the quinoa growing regions of the Andes, and in particular to the Altiplano of Bolivia where the highest quality quinoa, called *quinua real,* or royal quinoa, comes from. The Valley is at only 7,000 to 8,000 feet elevation, compared to the Altiplano at 12,000 to 14,000 feet, but it was the best match they could find.

This is where they planted the quinoa I sent Don, but their plans came to naught. Unfortunately, Don failed to mention that he wanted quinoa seed for planting. The quinoa I sent him was for eating, so it had been washed to remove the saponin. When quinoa is washed, if it is left too long in contact with water, the germination process begins. Afterward, when it's dried, the seed is killed. The quinoa I sent him had died and wouldn't germinate. It wasn't suitable for planting.

By 1982, I'd been living in Chile for about two years. The Pinochet regime still held control of the country with a tight fist. When I first arrived, I felt comfortable and relaxed. I was my usual easy-going self, but after a while I no longer felt that way. The constricted social atmosphere of the country under the Pinochet dictatorship had gotten under my skin. Chile was slowly changing me.

During those years there were nighttime curfews in Santiago. We might be at a party at someone's house, and then all of a sudden at 8:00 PM everything stopped, and everyone left quickly in order to get home by the imposed curfew hour. If you didn't leave in time, you were forced to spend the night wherever you were. Sometimes that meant sleeping on the floor in a place you'd rather not be.

One of the articles I wrote for *Clan* magazine reflected the general atmosphere in Chile at that time. Called "The Wiggle in the Walk," it was about my observation that Chileans didn't move their hips at all when they walked down the street. They were literally uptight, as if they were afraid that "big brother" was watching everything they did, even out on the streets.

During my last year there, Paz and I took a three-day bus trip to Rio de Janeiro in Brazil to experience Carnival. When the bus was passing through Chile, everyone sat quietly in their seats. In Argentina, people were even quieter. But when we crossed the border into Brazil, *caipirinha* drinks appeared out of nowhere, guitars came out, and the fun began; it was non-stop party time on the bus. And in Rio, everyone was totally relaxed, happy, free and more than a little crazy. *Why was I still living in the gray world of Chile?*

I realized I'd become so used to being uptight that I stopped noticing the many not-so-bright-looking young men in the Santiago streets with loaded machine guns in their arms. When I first arrived in Santiago, I never walked by a machine gun without feeling a chill run through my body. By 1982 I didn't even see them. It was definitely time to leave, so I booked a flight back to the States.

Don wrote me another letter. He said he wanted to try growing quinoa again in Colorado, so before leaving Chile, I had to find live seed for Don's second attempt. I put the word out that I was looking for quinoa seed and waited. As was often the case in South America, there were delays and miscommunications, and none of the people I had asked for seed had delivered any. My departure date for the States was fast approaching.

I had no quinoa seed. Without it, there would be no test planting in Colorado for another year. And then, once again, the unexpected happened. The evening before my plane was to leave, a close friend of Pilar Valdes, Kai Peronard, knocked on my door.

Kai was holding a fifteen-pound bag of beautiful multicolored quinoa seed from an obscure but picturesque village in the Chilean Andes called Isluga. He handed me the bag. I offered to pay him for the seed, but his humility forbade him from taking money, so in exchange I offered Kai the American-made shirt I was wearing. It was a nice shirt, one of my favorites, but nothing special. He loved it, and it turned out to be a most fortunate trade for me and for quinoa.

I literally traded the shirt off my back for the seed that led to opening the door to quinoa finally being released from centuries of obscurity.

The next day I flew to Denver, dropped the bag of seed off with Don in the airport, and continued on to Boston.

The First Quinoa Harvest

The quinoa seed I brought from Chile went from Don's hands to David's, and then to David Marsh, a farmer from the town of Center in the San Luis Valley of Colorado. The two Davids knew each other through the many agricultural development projects Cusack ran in the Valley. He convinced David Marsh to lend us some land for our experiment.

We made our quinoa trial one of David's projects for area farmers, and administered it through his non-profit, Sierra Blanca Associates. He got meager, though sufficient, funding through foundation grants to Sierra Blanca, and with that money we covered all the planting expenses. We had the land, the seed, and some money. With great expectations in our hearts we sowed five acres of the quinoa from Isluga. This time the seed germinated, and the young plants started growing without any problems.

I was traveling around in the United States, catching up with friends and visiting places I hadn't been to for over two years.

Don and I next saw each other later that summer at an Arica reunion held at the Sugar Maples resort in upstate New York. Paz was with me by then, and Don suggested we move to Boulder. He wanted us to start the quinoa project. He generously offered to pay me back what I'd lost in our failed Lambsbread Woolens venture with the money he was making from his advertising business. *Excellent,* I thought. *Let's do it!* Paz and I moved to Boulder and rented a one-room attic apartment on Walnut Street.

Paz was trilingual, in Spanish, English, and French, and she quickly got a job as a secretary at IBM. I went to Don's office and began work on our quinoa project, using about a one-square-foot corner of his desk.

Our crop in the Valley grew and came to harvest. I vividly recall driving through the San Luis Valley in October of that season. All of the barley destined to become Coors beer had been harvested, and acres of potato fields were being dug up. The autumn frosts had begun. The predominant colors were browns, yellows and golds, the post-harvest colors of earth and straw.

As we approached the quinoa test plots we were greeted by majestic seven-foot-tall plants, still green and growing, with heads full of pink and cream-colored seeds. Quinoa was the only green living plant in the entire Valley.

The word "miracle" once again entered my mind.

The San Luis Valley was chosen because of its apparent similarity to the quinoa growing regions in the Andes, but quite frankly, this was as much an aesthetic determination as it was a scientific one. We were just guessing, and we guessed correctly.

As far as we knew, this was the first time anyone had succeeded in growing quinoa to maturity outside the Andes, and we were ecstatic. We harvested and threshed the quinoa the same way the Andean peoples did, by hand. To get the saponin off in Bolivia they washed the seed in cold mountain streams. We filled big buckets with seed and water, agitated them, then poured the soapy water off and refilled the buckets. We did this over and over until the bitterness and foam were gone. Finally we cooked and then ate the first quinoa grown in Colorado. It was more than delicious; it filled us with optimism and joy.

This unusual success, which happened against all odds, gave us the encouragement we needed at the time. Others had tried to grow quinoa outside of her homeland and had failed. Had we failed, we certainly would have given up working with quinoa, but quinoa was good to us that year. She told us to keep going, to move on to the next step.

Quinoa is not that easy to grow. In all the years since our first crop, there have been only partial successes in Colorado. Yet in that year, we had luck on our side. Or perhaps it was fate, or something else.

The bottom line is that our Colorado test plantings in the summer of 1982 broke through the myth that had kept quinoa

Dave with harvested quinoa

out of our hands and palates for centuries. Quinoa will grow outside of the Andes.

Quinoa Corporation is Born

By the fall of 1982 we had proven that quinoa could grow in Colorado, but there was still no business, no company. All we had was a so-called agricultural development project. The first stage of our dream to introduce quinoa to the world outside the Andes took place under the auspices of David's Sierra Blanca Associates in Boulder, Colorado.

Don and I attended David's meetings with his other associates at Sierra Blanca. Peter Drake dropped out since there wasn't much else he could do for the project. The meetings dealt with many Sierra Blanca issues, such as the wool and potato projects, as well as internal management and funding problems, none of which were of any interest to Don or me. Each meeting seemed to go on forever, with little getting accomplished.

With David in charge of the meetings, it seemed like all that was going on was talk, talk, talk, and more talk. Don and

I quickly became frustrated by the lack of action.

After a few months of this, we dropped back from David's group and started working on our own, in our own way. Don and I talked a lot about what we should do. We came to agree that the only way quinoa was going to get anywhere was if we could turn it into a business. *Make quinoa a business, a money-making business, and all the pieces were sure to come together. Motivate people with the prospect of making money and they would act, not just talk.* I was convinced that business could serve as the vehicle to get us to our goal of seeing quinoa known and used throughout the world. And business was what Don really wanted to do. So, I bought a book on how to write a business plan, and we wrote one as best we could.

Although our plan was based on the concept that our quinoa would be grown in the United States, we were well aware that it might be years until that could become a reality. Experts told us that it can take as long as ten years to bring a new crop up to commercial scale. At that point, we had only grown and harvested one crop. So we included in our business plan the idea of "seeding" the market with imported quinoa. We planned to introduce quinoa to people during the first few years using as yet undetermined South American sources of supply. As quinoa was totally unknown in the States at that time, we also recognized that marketing would be a slow process. We hoped that by the time the market reached a commercially viable size, the domestically produced quinoa would be available for us to sell. We never intended to rely on importations forever.

Our first official shipment was a fifty-kilo sack from Bolivia on March 7, 1983. It cost us all of $164. Don recalls that the U.S. Customs Service, and possibly the DEA, were very curious about the nature of our product. There were so many probe holes in the bag that grain was flowing out freely from all sides.

Don and I collected a little venture capital from friends and found a lawyer to incorporate us. On June 16, 1983, which just happened to be my 41st birthday, Quinoa Corporation was born, with David, Don and myself as the principal shareholders.

Don never liked David; they had very little in common. I liked just about everyone, but when it came to David, I wasn't exactly sure. Yes, I liked him, but with difficulty. Don and I included David in the company because we felt we needed him. He was managing the test plantings of quinoa in Colorado, and he also had years of experience and good contacts in South America. Of even greater importance was the fact that he could travel to South America on funding provided from Sierra Blanca donors, whereas our Corporation had almost nothing in the way of financial resources. We were a typical high-risk, undercapitalized garage startup. Our first quinoa had to come from Bolivia or Peru, and David was the best person to go there and get it. So, despite some personal reluctance on our parts, we invited David in as an equal partner.

Don and I decided that I would be the president and he the treasurer. It was an arbitrary decision, as in reality we considered ourselves equal partners, and, for the most part, everything we did was by mutual consent. It was obvious that Don had more business sense, and his word in deciding practical matters carried more weight than mine. He was completely in charge of decisions regarding sales and marketing.

I was the visionary of the company, and more of a public figure. I was the one most involved with the product itself. I loved quinoa and knew the most about it from a technical point of view, all the way from seed selection to development of recipes. My wide range of experience with quinoa included such oddities as squatting for hours under the hot sun in a dusty field emasculating tiny quinoa flowers with the point of a needle. It was something one does during breeding experiments. Never in my life had I ever imagined doing anything like that.

Our two positions in the new company also seemed to flow from something in our personalities, with me being more outgoing than Don, and once we decided who was to be what, we never questioned what we had done.

By this time our friendship had developed to the point that it seemed as if we were thinking each other's thoughts. Don and I liked each other from the very beginning, and through our years together we reached a rare level of trust and mutual respect. When it came time for us to apply ourselves to quinoa we worked in perfect harmony. We were the perfect team.

David remained as president of Sierra Blanca Associates and was not an officer of Quinoa Corporation. We put one of David's consultants at Sierra Blanca, Kevin McCullough, a smart tough-looking guy who looked the part of a real businessman, on our Board of Directors. Kevin had an MBA from Harvard Business School, and we gratefully turned to him whenever we needed to know what "real" businesses would do.

Don and I thought long and hard about what to name the company, and in the end we chose what was most direct and simple, Quinoa Corporation.

One of the issues we confronted right at the beginning was the spelling of quinoa. In most Latin American countries, quinoa is spelled with a "u," not an "o," before the "a." Thus, in Bolivia and Peru, the main producer countries, it is spelled *"quinua."* Only in Chile is it spelled "quinoa," and the scientific name is also spelled with an "o" (*Chenopodium quinoa* Willd).

Don and I decided to spell it "quinoa" for two reasons. The first was purely aesthetic. Don simply thought the word looked better with the "o." The second reason was that we didn't want to market quinoa as another Latin American ethnic food. Don didn't want to see quinoa sold only in bodegas or specialty shops like yucca, nopales (cactus), or adobo (seasoning). Although we felt deep respect for quinoa's Andean origins, we had another, more forward-looking, vision for her.

In our minds, quinoa was to become a food for everyone throughout the world to enjoy without any limitations or baggage attached to it. We were going to grow it in the United States. It would be a totally new food, with such outstanding nutritional properties and culinary possibilities that it could truly be called a super food. Toward that end, Don coined the term "supergrain" to apply to quinoa.

David continued trying to make quinoa a viable crop for Colorado farmers. Having satisfied ourselves that quinoa would grow in Colorado, during the 1983 planting season we tested forty-eight different varieties on about fifty acres in over twelve locations. From this experiment, only six varieties succeeded in Colorado, and the range of suitable locations was slightly expanded. Six varieties may not sound like a lot, but it was definitely enough to encourage further experimentation. During that year, Dr. Duane Johnson, a professor of agronomy at Colorado State University, enthusiastically joined forces with us and started his own test plantings.

With planting activity well under way in Colorado, David arranged with Dr. Mario Tapia to collect and send a small shipment of quinoa from Peru. This quinoa was gathered by Dr. Tapia's nephew and stored in his living room before shipment. It was the first of many multi-sack shipments of quinoa we would eventually import and sell from South America.

In January of 1984 we tried to raise $775,000 through an "Offering Memorandum" that Don and I wrote up with the legal guidance of a retired SEC lawyer in Denver. It was a complicated fifty-six page document that took us months to produce, and it resulted in absolutely nothing. Since we didn't get anything near the required minimum investment amount we weren't able to use any of the money pledged to us.

Then the unthinkable happened!

David

Despite our thoroughly reasoned decision to include David in Quinoa Corporation, relations between David and Don and myself were never harmonious. Don and David had very different personal styles and interests. They hardly ever talked or did anything together unless it was absolutely necessary. I had a great deal of respect for David's intelligence, work and accomplishments, and I tried to be his friend, but I found it difficult relating to him. There was something about his attitude that tried my patience. Talking to him felt a lot like talking to a wall. Even though I had my problems with David I always knew that he was a good person, and I recognized that many, many people loved him.

One of our problems was that David wore two distinct hats, one as head of Sierra Blanca Associates and the other as our partner in Quinoa Corporation. Don and I never knew for sure which hat he had on. It seemed that his first priority was always Sierra

Blanca, understandably, and that he didn't care that much about Quinoa Corporation. Within our company, I'm sure he felt a little like the odd man out, as Don and I were obviously close personal friends and often functioned as if with one voice.

We found ourselves fighting over nearly every decision, with Don and me on one side, and David on the other. As time went on it only seemed to get worse.

One of our earliest disagreements was over how to spell the word quinoa. Whereas Don and I preferred quinoa with an "o," David preferred the more ethnically correct spelling, "*quinua.*" We knew this was not a decision to be made lightly. Whatever we decided at that point in time would become the standard spelling for quinoa in all the non-Andean world. Don and I had two votes to David's one, so we prevailed.

The next big issue, of equal importance, was how the word quinoa would be pronounced. We saw right away that most people would need to be taught how to pronounce quinoa. Just looking at the word gives little clue as to how to say it. David wanted people to pronounce the three syllables distinctly, as in "key nu ah" (accent on the "key" with "nu" and "ah" very quickly slurred together). Although this was perhaps technically accurate, Don and I were sure that it would be misleading, as people might tend to put the accent in the wrong place, on the "nu," instead of the "key."

I spent many hours discussing this with Paz, a native Spanish speaker. We decided to explain the pronunciation with only two syllables, as in "keen wa." This was closer to what it actually sounded like when an average South American said the word.

David disagreed and we went our separate ways on this issue. Don and I used the more practical two syllable guide to pronunciation in all the Quinoa Corporation literature, and David used the three syllable version in Sierra Blanca literature. Sure enough, many people followed David and wound up saying it the wrong way, as "key nú ah." That legacy exists even today.

It didn't matter what David and I talked about, we almost always ended up in conflict. At one point, recognizing that we would never argue our way to agreement, I thought we should try doing something together that we could both agree on. At the time we both trusted in the guidance of "throwing the I Ching," so we agreed to meet at my apartment and do a joint I Ching, each of us throwing the coins to indicate alternate lines and determine a reading. How did it work out? After a few minutes alone together, David stormed out, I followed, and found myself standing in the middle of Walnut Street yelling my head off at him.

After that meltdown I saw that no matter how hard we tried to reach common ground, it simply wasn't going to work. Our company was almost a year old, and we were already trapped in an impossible situation. The three of us just couldn't get along together, but we needed each other. *We're stuck. What can we do?*

After one particularly contentious Quinoa Corporation board meeting in May 1984, during which David didn't agree with anything we suggested, Don and I walked out of the office we were using as a makeshift headquarters in a cloud of total frustration. As we hit the street I turned to him and said ...

"There's only one solution."

As these words tumbled out of my mouth, my hand formed a gun, like the ones we used as kids when we wanted to play cowboys and Indians but didn't have any toy guns to use. The index and middle finger form the barrel and the thumb serves as the hammer. The two smallest fingers curl toward the palm to complete the look.

I cocked the hammer and shot it off.

Don knew exactly what I meant. My words and my gesture symbolized our shared feelings of frustration with David, our confusion as to what to do, and our sense of being caught in a hopeless situation.

I will never *ever* forget that moment.

Shortly after that meeting, on May 21, 1984, David left on a trip to South America to attend an international conference on Andean affairs, as well as to meet people about Sierra Blanca's projects, including quinoa.

On Saturday, June 2nd, Alfalfa's, Boulder's largest natural food supermarket, had us present quinoa at their in-store demo kiosk. This was to be our big chance. Up until that time we had been selling small amounts of quinoa directly to people we expected would like it. One such group were the followers of Michio Kushi, the macrobiotic diet people, and yes, they loved it. But thus far, we had never presented quinoa to the general public. This was our opportunity to debut quinoa.

At Alfalfa's we served little paper cups of cooked quinoa, and also fried quinoa balls, much like falafel (See Recipe, pg. 198). Don and I wore aprons printed with our logo. We handed out information flyers and recipe booklets, and I talked and talked for hours about my favorite subject. At the end of a very long day, the bulk bins of quinoa at Alfalfa's were sold out. Quinoa was a smashing success!

Sunday morning, my energies drained from so much talk with so many people, I needed to go on retreat. I locked the door of our one room apartment, unplugged the phone, and prepared the space for a one day meditation retreat. I was home alone, as Paz was visiting with her sister in Houston. To clear and "purify" the space I burned some incense. I put resin balls of frankincense and myrrh on a small square of copper heated red hot over a burner on the stove. This should have spread fragrant wisps of smoke gently throughout the room. Much to my chagrin, the resin caught fire and spread tiny droplets of black ash over the whole room. Instead of "purifying" the space, I had inadvertently done the exact opposite.

My retreat did not go smoothly. I did meditate, but I did not reach the depth of tranquility I was accustomed to. Something felt wrong—very, very wrong.

David's trip included stops in Miami, Colombia, Ecuador, Peru, and finally Bolivia. The trip was paid for with Sierra Blanca funds and was for Sierra Blanca business, but he was also going to look for supplies of quinoa that we might import. He was supposed to go on to Chile, but a flight cancellation kept David an extra day in Bolivia and allowed him the free time to go as a tourist to the Tiahuanaco pre-Columbian archeological site seventy-two kilometers west of La Paz, near the shores of Lago Titicaca. That day was Sunday, June 3, 1984.

Tiahuanaco

As he sat on the top of a hill covering the Akapana Pyramid in the middle of the ruin site, he wrote a letter to Florence

View from Akapana Hill

Magneron, his girlfriend at that time:

> "Noon, Tiawanacu. Just for a moment I write a few lines here at this legendary birthplace of civilization . . . The land, the clear sky and floating clouds, the wind through the dry grass, the cracked red earth, and the monoliths of a distant past . . . I feel very peaceful here. Time stops. I almost did not make it here. I have passed several times on route from Puno to La Paz. But luck said, 'yes' this time. Some day perhaps we can come here together. If so destined. Autumn soon winter. The wind spirit whispers to me, au revoir."

A few moments later, some young tourists from Great Britain heard David shout and saw him running down the hill, falling and rolling over several times until he lay motionless on his back. They assumed he had suffered a heart attack due to the high altitude and tried to revive him with CPR, to no avail. One of the group of about a dozen tourists at the site went to the nearby town to fetch Severo Chávez, the local doctor. Chávez examined David and shook his head, exclaiming *"Murió, está muerto."* (He died. He's dead.) It was 1:30 PM.

Back in Boulder, I was in the middle of my meditation retreat.

When they then lifted David's lifeless body and placed it face down on a blanket, one of the tourists noticed something totally unexpected. On the back of David's sweater under his left shoulder was some blood. On closer inspection they saw what looked very much like a bullet hole!

That discovery got everyone's attention, and the local constable was immediately summoned to the scene. He did what he could to investigate what had happened. Starting that day, and over the course of the next few days, investigations were conducted by the La Paz police; the national police, known as the *Division de Investigación Nacional* or DIN; by Royce Fichte, the American consul in La Paz; and by Peter McFarren, an Associated Press correspondent.

The evidence showed that David had been shot in the back by a copper-clad .22 caliber bullet, presumably from a rifle, and that it had pierced his aorta and killed him. It is not easy to kill a person with such a small caliber, low energy bullet unless it hits vital organs. The bullet that killed David did just that.

Curiously, none of the tourists at the site reported hearing a shot being fired. Up on the Altiplano, at high altitudes where the air is thin, sound travels far. There were no city noises, no highway traffic, no noises of any kind. It was dead quiet at Tiahuanaco that day, as it is every day. You could hear a pin drop, yet no one heard a gun go off. There was no evidence of robbery. There was no one with a gun within the fenced-in ruin site. No one had exited through the only gate. Among the tourists who were in the compound, no suspect was identified.

The official conclusion, that reached by DIN, was that David had been hit by a hunter's stray bullet.

Back in Boulder, in the evening of that fateful Sunday, having given up on my retreat, I plugged the phone back in. I received a call from Paz, who had heard from David's ex-wife Silvia earlier in the day. She told me the shocking news.

"David is dead!"

Nobody was satisfied with the explanation offered by DIN, and speculation on the real cause of David's death flourished for many years thereafter. Royce Fichte, the American consul, although he thought the investigation "as thorough as possible, given the police capabilities," called the stray bullet theory "a convenient answer, but a remote possibility."

Some people back in Boulder assumed it was a simple robbery gone bad, but that did not fit the facts. Others thought that David must have stumbled onto a drug processing operation. That did not fit the facts either. The most interesting explanation for what happened was that David was assassinated by the CIA. The theory was that David had himself been in the CIA and was about to reveal secret information about the CIA's involvement in the overthrow of the Allende government in Chile. David had been in Chile at the time of the Pinochet coup and the subject was one of great interest to him. Though a compelling theory, once again there were no facts to support it.

To this day, no one knows exactly how or why David was killed.

The most disturbing conclusion Don and I had to consider was that David had been shot because of what we were doing with quinoa. How or why this might be true was not at all obvious. But if it were true, we were not only in a mess, we were in a very dangerous mess.

David's body was returned to Colorado on June 9th and was buried in Woodland Park Cemetery two days later. He was 40 years old.

David F. Cusack

Don and I were stunned, I especially, because of what I had said a few short weeks earlier about the "only solution." *Did I somehow wish David dead? No, certainly not. But, why did I say what I said? Did I know that David was going to be shot? Why had my meditation retreat been so weird?* Not only was it on the same day as David's death, it was during the same few hours. I was in shock, and thoroughly confused. I had no idea what had just happened, nor why. *Was I in some way responsible?* That awful possibility haunted me for years afterward.

Aside from the emotional impact of David's death, Don and I had doubts about whether we should continue the business. We wondered if this was a sign for us to drop our crazy dream.

There were many practical consequences to losing David. *Could we continue even if we wanted to?* David was our link to South America and all potential sources of supply. David spoke Spanish. David had Sierra Blanca funds that allowed him to travel. David had the connections to farmers in the San Luis Valley.

Don and I were at a loss as to what to do with David when he was alive. We needed him, and he was impossible to work with. Now that we didn't have him, we didn't know what to do without him.

CHAPTER THREE

Quinoa Moves On

AFTER DAVID DIED WE PROBABLY would have decided to quit working with quinoa if people hadn't started showing up at our office encouraging us to continue. The headline in the local Boulder newspaper read "Boulder Professor Shot in Bolivia." Everyone was talking about the death. There was a flood of positive feeling released in the Boulder and Denver communities for David, but also for us and for quinoa. It felt as if we were being swept along by a force greater than ourselves.

People we didn't know came to talk to us. Some offered to help, and some just said that we had to continue our business if only for David's sake. As it turned out, none of the offers of help actually materialized, but the encouraging words did have their intended effect. We felt as if we had to continue.

Fortunately for us and for quinoa, Dr. John McCamant stepped in to take over the Colorado growing project that David started. John was a professor of political science at the University of Denver's Graduate School for International Studies and was David's Ph.D. advisor and close friend. He caught the quinoa "bug" after a meeting we had with him in August 1983.

In an email to me dated August 1997 John wrote:

"It was fourteen years ago this month when you, David, and Mario Tapia visited me on the way back from Malachite. I have been reflecting on that visit because it is now clear that that was when the burden of quinoa was laid on me. I was puzzled by the visit at the time because I did not know why you were coming here and telling me all about quinoa. You probably did not know either."

John became the new president at Sierra Blanca Associates. He dropped all other activities and concentrated on managing the quinoa test plantings in the San Luis Valley. He did so year after year, despite great adversity. John was to become one of a small group of truly dedicated lovers of quinoa, and he continued as such until the day he died on May 6, 2015.

With the efforts to develop a quinoa crop in Colorado in the capable hands of John McCamant, and also Duane Johnson and later Sarah Ward, both professors of agronomy at Colorado State University, Don and I turned our attention to the importation and marketing operations at Quinoa Corporation. We knew that it could take many years for domestic supply to kick in, but we hoped that luck would be on our side. While we waited, we planned to "seed" the marketplace with imported quinoa.

After David was killed in Bolivia, and Don and I decided to continue with Quinoa Corporation, we had to figure out how to get our hands on quinoa in South America. We needed a replacement for David as supply manager. There were only two of us left, so one of us had to do it, and that meant one of us would eventually have to go down there. Which one of us would it be? Don and I looked at each other.

Don spoke first.

"I'm not going! I do sales and marketing. Besides you're married to a Chilean and have been there many times."

I answered.

"Me? Ohhh, no! Are you crazy? We don't know why David was murdered, do we? Maybe it was because of quinoa. You know that. Sorry, my dear friend. If you think I'm willingly walking into some sort of death trap in Bolivia, you must be out of your freakin' mind."

Don won.

It made sense that the task of finding quinoa to import should fall to me. I had lived two years in South America, spoke a little Spanish, and I was relatively comfortable traveling under difficult circumstances. And I guess I was maybe a bit less risk-averse than Don.

The strange thing is that once that job was put in my hands, it developed with a speed and ease that none of us could have imagined. Not only that, everything Don and I now did seemed to work like magic. Something had changed! At one point I had the perhaps crazy idea that David had been some sort of martyr in the cause of quinoa, that his life had been "sacrificed" by the powers that be, in order for new energy to flow into quinoa's mission. That everything got better after David's death was obvious. How or why this happened, I do not pretend to know.

Up until this point, Quinoa Corporation had been a business in name only. Nothing much had happened. Don and I worked out of a small office on Walnut Street, close to the foothills on the edge of Boulder. Don was busy running his advertising business in the main room. I had a small room in the back where we stored the first sacks of grain that came in. But there wasn't that much to do.

At first we sold the little quinoa we had in twenty-five pound bags. Eventually we created the first packaged quinoa, a simple cellophane bag with a stick-on label that we designed ourselves. One-pound packages were made, as well as a single-serving size to give away as samples. All of this was done by hand, and often the labels were a bit crooked.

We tried to make our labels simple, clear and direct, laboring over the exact form of the "Q" to use. Don ultimately chose the typeface. We did a drawing of the quinoa plant and laughed a lot because one of the leaves inadvertently looked just like a chicken head. Don borrowed a teal green color scheme for our label from an Aveda shampoo bottle. He liked the colors, not realizing how unusual they were for a food product in those times. The odd colors and graphics were so distinctive that several years later they won a design prize. And one of our suppliers later pirated our label, down to the smallest detail, including the chicken head, for use in his own country.

After David's death our business started growing. Later in the year, anticipating the day when we would be receiving container-loads of quinoa, we moved to a warehouse in the industrial area

Our first label

on the other side of town. To finance the move we looked for more investors, and found a few. John McCamant was one; the others were friends of Don's and friends of friends. We seemed to get everything we needed exactly when we needed it, but nothing extra.

For the first time, I had my own office, with my own desk and chairs. Don had his, and besides the small warehouse space in the back, we also had a reception area and a kitchen. We also began hiring employees, a receptionist, and someone part-time to work in the back. Finally we were starting to look like a real business.

At the beginning, the only equipment we had in the back were a bathroom-type scale, a large scoop, and a device for sewing up the twenty-five pound paper bags. We filled the bags by hand with the scoop and weighed each one on the scale, adding just a little more to make sure we didn't cheat anyone. We contracted out the filling of the one-pound cellophane packages to a local nut company and received them neatly stacked in cases. Later we started using pallets, and had to buy a pallet mover. Still later we bought a forklift truck and put up racks on the walls for holding pallets full of product.

Quinoa from South America came to us via ocean freight and then by truck from the port of Houston to Boulder. It was always in woven polypropylene bags imprinted with names of products we'd never heard of. Quinoa wasn't yet important enough to have its own name printed on a bag, so the ones they used were second hand. In the beginning we unloaded the trucks by ourselves, by hand. The bags each weighed about a hundred pounds and were difficult to handle.

Don and I worked hard, physically and otherwise. As is often the case with fledgling businesses, there was a stressful level of responsibility now that we had investors watching our progress or lack thereof.

But it was fun, and thrilling, too, after so many years, to finally see quinoa coming into the United States. This miraculous super food, as we had always thought of it, was finally making its way into the homes of American families.

Quinoa, a World Class Grain

An Aymara child with a beautiful smile

The desk in my sparse office was placed so I could look out the windows. Behind me, taped to the wall, were two huge maps, one of South America, and the other of Bolivia. Referring to them I could see in great detail exactly where everything related to supply was happening. On the side wall were two large poster photos, one of a typical Bolivian indigenous woman, and the other of an indigenous child with a big, beautiful smile. It was important for me to feel the presence of the original people of quinoa in my Boulder workspace. They represented quinoa's ancient and humble past.

On the corner of my desk I taped a chart from the Food and Agriculture Organization of the United Nations. The chart showed all the major food commodities listed in order of total quantity produced worldwide in 1984 (in millions of metric tons).

"Sugar cane 929.76; Wheat 512.33; Rice 462.27; Maize 450.44; Sugar beet 296.35; Potatoes 290.94; Barley 169.43; Cassava 133.23; Sweet potatoes 133.03; Vegetables (fresh) 112.35;

Soybeans 90.75; Sorghum 70.70; Grapes 64.51; Tomatoes 64.08; Oats 46.20; Cabbages (and brassicas) 41.48; Apples 39.81"

I put this chart on my desktop so I would see it each and every day, to remind me of my goal for quinoa's future. I knew deep in my heart that one day quinoa would be on this list. It might not be in my lifetime, but I knew it was inevitable. Quinoa is too good not to find its rightful place among the world's major foodstuffs. Worldwide quinoa production in 1983 was only 20,362 metric tons. In 2015 it was it was already 238,000 metric tons, but still far short of my goal.

Grains—wheat, rice, maize (corn), barley—were up near the top of the list. This made sense to me, as grains have always been the staples of the world's food supply. There's been a trend lately to call quinoa a seed and not a grain. Wikipedia defines food grains as "small, hard, dry seeds, with or without attached hulls or fruit layers, harvested for human or animal consumption." The word "grain" is not a scientific term, so it can not be defined in any precise way. Whether something is a grain or not is really a matter of practicality or common sense. To my way of thinking, quinoa is a grain.

From a practical perspective, grains are seeds of food plants that can be grown in great quantity on large area farms, are easily harvested by combines, and cleaned with machines. Grains are durable and easy to store for long periods of time. They are also easy to transport long distances, for example on ships or trains. Grains differ from beans and legumes in that they contain a higher percentage of carbohydrate. Beans tend to have a higher percentage of protein. Grains can also be distinguished from other foodstuffs in how they are prepared, cooked, and eaten. Unlike other types of seeds, they are often ground into flour and used for baking or made into pasta. And of course, grains are used for making beer.

Quinoa meets all these criteria. They say that "if it looks like a duck, walks like a duck, and quacks like a duck, it is probably a duck." Quinoa is a grain.

What tends to confuse people is that most well known grains, like wheat, rice, corn, barley, rye, and millet, are caryopses, that is, seeds of grass plants. Quinoa is not. It is from a broadleaf plant, as are amaranth and buckwheat. In terms of how they are grown, stored, transported, and used, they should all be considered grains.

Calling quinoa a seed and not a grain doesn't make sense to me. It provides no useful information, no distinction from other seeds. Quinoa is of course a seed, but so are all the other grains, and all the beans, many nuts, and even coconuts. Think about it. Quinoa is much more like rice or wheat than it is like a sunflower, sesame, or tomato seed. Some people believe seeds have more food value than grains. The association of grains with carbohydrate, undesirable in some fad diets, may also be a factor in why people want to call quinoa a seed and not a grain. Quinoa is a grain, a stereotype-breaking grain.

An interesting fact about quinoa is that it can be used in any of the ways other grains are used. Don and I purposely wanted to prevent quinoa being seen only as a traditional food with defined uses. Most grains are prepared in rather standardized and limiting ways. Rice is usually prepared as a dish by itself, as a "bowl of rice," or as a side dish. Most wheat is ground into flour for bread, baked goods, or pasta. It is rarely eaten as a "bowl of wheat," although it could be. Oats are usually rolled and eaten as a breakfast cereal. Barley is almost always made into beer or used as a soup ingredient. In fact, all of these grains can be used in all these various ways, but tradition has determined how most of us think of them, and how we use them.

Tradition plays a huge role in how we use food; it determines the recipes people use, day after day. Quinoa has its traditional uses in South America, but in other parts of the world it is too new to be associated with any one type of use. The wonderful thing about quinoa is that it can be used successfully as a whole grain dish, in breads, pasta, baked goods, breakfast cereals, soups, and even in beer making. And as far as recipes are concerned, quinoa is only limited by the creativity of the person cooking it.

This point about the power of tradition was dramatically brought home to me when I was staying with a family in a rather poor neighborhood in Lima, Peru. I suggested to the women of the family that we cook some quinoa. They prepared *locro de quinua* (See Recipe, pg. 199), a traditional dish that can best be described as creamed quinoa stew. It was quite delicious, and I ate a lot of it.

Afterwards, I suggested that we prepare a meal with quinoa as it is done in the United States. I thought they would be interested in trying different styles of serving quinoa. I cooked it as a dry fluffy whole grain dish (See Recipe, pg. 193), much like rice, used as an accompaniment for a vegetable dish with some sort of sauce. This is probably the most common way quinoa is prepared in the United States. I also served it in a vegetable soup (See Recipe, pg. 200) and as crispy little deep-fried croquettes (See Recipe, pg. 201).

The dishes were excellent and very tasty, but nobody in the family wanted to eat them. The women at least tried each one. The men refused. They seemed scared to even taste dishes that were too strange, too different from what they were used to. Such is the power of tradition.

Since outside of South America there are no traditional uses or recipes for quinoa, many people have created totally new quinoa dishes. Innovation with quinoa in kitchens throughout the world is already happening.

Of course there are other more complex ways that grains are used. Corn is used to make oil and starch as well as industrial chemicals. Quinoa could easily be used as a high quality oil crop, considering its unusually high percentage of oil (5.3 to 8.4%). The yield in terms of oil produced per acre of such a crop would exceed by up to twenty times the yield of corn.

Quinoa starch has unusual properties which could have important industrial uses. The size of the starch granule is ten to twenty times smaller than that of corn or wheat. Saponin, a by-product of quinoa, has interesting potential uses as well. For example, it can be used anywhere foam or suds are needed, as in soaps or shampoo. To date very little work has been done on producing and using any of quinoa's components. The main reasons are the high cost of quinoa compared to other commodities and the relative lack of reliable high volume production. This will certainly change.

Dirt, Dust, and Little Stones

One of our chief concerns about importing quinoa from South America was the standard of cleanliness and purity of the product. Aricans, we learned, had attempted to import quinoa for sale just to the members of the Arica School in the early 70's. They managed to get some Bolivian quinoa shipped to New

York, but it was contaminated with so many little stones and pieces of glass that they dared not sell it.

Don and I recognized that it would be a disaster for us to sell anything that wasn't completely free of foreign material. In the U.S. we expect all our food to be clean. But in those days perfectly clean quinoa just did not exist in South America. What were we to do?

We were terrified by the possibility of someone breaking a tooth on a hidden stone. Don insisted, "That would surely be the end of us!" We knew this was a serious issue, and one that would not be easily resolved.

When we started our business, there was no commercial infrastructure for producing or handling quinoa. It was grown in Bolivia and Peru on small farms, almost exclusively for use by members of the indigenous communities. Small quantities were sent to the cities to be sold at street markets, but none of it was meant for export or even for food stores or restaurants; so cleanliness and purity of product was never really an issue.

Quinoa was produced using the most primitive traditional methods, and those methods unfortunately guaranteed that the end product would contain many contaminants. There was just

Threshing quinoa

Cleaning and winnowing quinoa

no other way available for poor people essentially trying to produce food for home use.

The Bolivian Altiplano citizens were generally organized into communities, with the members working together for the common good. Community land was prepared, quinoa was sown, tended, harvested, threshed, and winnowed, and all of this was done by hand. Harvested plants were laid on the ground, or on large plastic tarpaulins when available, and trucks were sometimes used to run over the dry plants to separate the grains from the seed heads. Grains were winnowed by tossing them up in the air and letting the wind blow the chaff away.

The communities also had to tackle the issue of saponin removal. The only method they knew was to wash the quinoa by hand in freezing cold streams, a job done almost exclusively by women. They then spread the wet quinoa out on the ground, or on tarpaulins, to dry in the sun. Again, dirt, stones, and worse wound up mixed in with the quinoa, and that was what we had shipped to us. We had no other option.

Starting in the early 70's several farmers cooperatives were formed, and they set themselves the goal of improving production methods for quinoa. They were of course interested in removing stones and foreign material from the grain and in mechanizing the saponin removal process, which was the most onerous of all. ANAPQUI (*Asociación Nacional de Productores de Quinua*), created in 1983, was the main organization of small producers, preceded by CECAOT (*Central de Cooperativas Agropecuarias Operación*

Early processing plant

Tierra), founded in 1974 by Jaime Alba. These organizations, and several others in Bolivia, built so-called processing plants, but none did what they were supposed to do. Ingo Junge tried to design a modern processing facility for quinoa in Chile but also failed.

In 1992 I was asked by the International Development Research Centre of Canada (IDRC) to study the current state of affairs of quinoa production and processing in Bolivia. In my report I made the following observations:

"The pilot plant was very well equipped with a solar toaster, dry scarifier, separator, water based stone remover, and washer. Drying was done on a concrete slab outside under the sun. Most of the machines were in line except for a break after the stone remover. Quinua had to then be carried by hand to the washer. This plant is the model for the six new plants to be built by the United Nations. Although the plant looks impressive, we did not find it at all efficient. It uses 50 liters of water for every kilo of quinua produced, indicating that the scarifier is not doing its job. The most poignant indication of the lack of effectiveness of this plant was the fact that at the end of this line of impressive machines was one lone woman sitting at a table picking stones and other debris out of the finished product. All of the 100MT/yr. would have to go through her hands in order for the quinua from this plant to meet export standards."

This sad situation was all they had in 1992, and it did not improve until much later when quinoa began to be recognized as a serious export crop. Once that happened, people were more willing to invest in proper machinery and methods. Today, most quinoa coming out of South America has the saponin removed and is cleaned and sometimes packaged before it is ever exported.

Working with quinoa in the mid 80's, we had to make do with whatever was available at the time. So we imported quinoa full of stones, dirt, dust, plant particles, pieces of metal, glass, unidentifiable objects, and yes, even rodent feces. They did the saponin removal in South America, but we had to do all the cleaning in Colorado.

Luckily we had Celestial Seasonings, the herbal tea company, as a neighbor, and we contracted with them to run all of our quinoa over their cleaning machinery, particularly their gravity table, an ingenious device that separates everything put on it according to its specific gravity. It worked, not perfectly, but good enough. Our biggest problem was with mouse droppings. As luck would have it they shared a similar specific gravity with quinoa grains, so we had to take extra special care to remove them.

Celestial sent us our cleaned quinoa in large fiber drums, which we then sent to the local nut company for packaging. Although the drums were heavy, we could roll them around tilted on edge. This simplified things tremendously. Some of the drums we kept in our back room, so we could hand scoop quinoa into our bulk bags.

Our First Supplier

As it turned out, our first big breakthrough in finding supply came through my wife, Paz. Her father, Sergio Huneeus, was a Chilean diplomat. He served for a while at the United Nations, and Paz and her brothers and sister spent their early years in New York. Sergio's most significant post, however, was as the Chilean Ambassador to Ecuador. During the years the family lived in Ecuador, Paz's sister Carmen Elena met and later married Enrique ("Capi") Espinosa Paez, an Ecuadorian land owner, businessman, farmer, and a true gentleman.

Capi knew who was doing what in agriculture and had high-level contacts throughout South America. Although I never directly asked him to find us quinoa, people in that world were curious and talking about what I was doing, and word got around. One of his acquaintances, a Peruvian named Alfonso Poblete Vidal, heard that I was interested in quinoa and started buying up supplies for me without my knowledge, let alone permission.

Poblete, like most Peruvians of his social class, knew little about quinoa, but he knew how to get things done in Peru, and he knew how to export. He became our first supplier, starting with one full container-load, with many others to follow. A standard twenty-foot shipping container held between eighteen and twenty metric tons of quinoa.

Alfonso was a large scale commercial farmer. His land was in Barranca, on the coast of Peru north of Lima, a place where quinoa did not traditionally grow. That didn't stop him from trying to grow it on his own land. In fact, he also tried growing coffee on his farm, something that had never been done before. That was the type of person Alfonso was, an innovative risk taker. Unfortunately, both projects failed.

Some of the quinoa he sold us was grown in the highlands of Peru, but most was part of the many thousands of tons of quinoa smuggled each year from Bolivia into Peru. Smuggling of quinoa between those two countries happens even today. Poblete bought quinoa from local traders, consolidated it, and sold it to us. The containers went by sea freight out of the Peruvian port of Callao, to the port of Houston, and then up to Boulder by truck.

Buying a container-load of quinoa from Peru involved a complex set of steps that we had to learn by trial and error. Contracts were almost always negotiated in person in South America. Official sales documents had to be written up, agreed to, and signed by parties on both sides. Our "sales contract" had a full page of legal conditions and disclaimers printed on the back. The truth is, we copied it from somewhere, and neither Don nor I understood anything it said. What was important was that it look good, and it did.

An "Irrevocable Payable on Sight Letter of Credit" had to be drawn up and opened in our bank in cooperation with a Peruvian bank. The name of that document always impressed me. The letter of credit guaranteed payment to the seller once he delivered certain documents to our bank. Those documents included a bill of lading stating that the container was indeed loaded on a ship headed our way, a bill of sale, a phytosanitary certificate issued by the Peruvian government, and an official certificate of country of origin. We had to learn to put all this together.

We also had to find and hire a shipping company as well as a customs broker to get our quinoa into the country. United States Customs officials of course had never heard of quinoa, so there was no official import code assigned to it. They called it "other," and always looked at it carefully before letting it in. In those days, all intercontinental communications were sent by telex, so we had a telex terminal installed in our office.

Aside from the logistical hurdles and paperwork nightmares, there was also the issue of the quinoa grain itself. Was it good quinoa? How clean was it? Had the saponin been reliably removed? What about the size of the grains, and the color? We were new at this, but so was Sr. Poblete. Some shipments went without a hitch, but not all. Usually I traveled to Peru to inspect the quinoa myself, before it was readied for shipment.

I loved those trips. I stayed in strange hotels in strange places, and ate strange food. During those days the infamous "*Sendero Luminoso*" (Shining Path) and the Túpac Amaru Revolutionary Movement guerrillas were still active, and we never knew when they'd blow up the electrical towers in Lima and leave us in darkness. It happened quite often. As a presumably wealthy CEO of an American corporation traveling in Peru, I also had to be wary of getting kidnapped. That, thank God, never happened. Who would have paid the ransom? I spent a lot of time with Poblete and his family, stayed with them on their farm in Barranca, and got to know them well.

At that time, the tools of my trade consisted of a strong magnifying glass and a small metal grain probe. The probe had a pointed end and was used to take grain samples through the woven polypropylene bags without damaging them. I probed bag after bag until I was satisfied that all the quinoa was ready for export. How did I test for saponin? I tasted it. If the quinoa was bitter, it was no good. I got to the point that I could also tell just by looking at the grains under the magnifier if they had saponin on them or not. One time I found an entire eighteen metric ton shipment inadequately cleaned of saponin, and I wouldn't let Poblete ship it to us. He had to resell it in the marketplaces of Peru.

Another time, a whole container of quinoa with saponin still on it arrived in the port of Houston. I hadn't been able to do an inspection before it left Peru. What a disaster! *What do we do now? Send it back? Who pays for it?* Given our tight money situation, we couldn't afford to take a loss of that size. We also didn't want to jeopardize our relationship with Poblete by shifting the burden onto him. A simple mistake was made, and it threw us into a very serious crisis.

We decided not to reject the container. Instead, we found a small independent rice processor in Louisiana, Shelton Fontineau, and sent the whole shipment to him to see if he could get the saponin off. It was an enormous gamble, and once again, luck was on our side. Fontineau managed to remove all the saponin from the quinoa using only an old fashioned rice polisher. This had never been done before.

Rice polishing machinery looks like a long fat tube. It removes the bran, the outer layers of a rice grain, by either rubbing the grains against an abrasive material on the inside surfaces of the tube, or by rubbing the grains against each other. Fontineau's machine rubbed the grains against each other. With quinoa this has to be done very, very gently, and with a great deal of control, since the quinoa germ wraps around the outside of the grain. If you knock the germ off, you lose the part of the grain with the most nutrition. The trick is to rub off the saponin, but not break the germ off. Fontineau did it. He proved that it can be done.

This simple feat was an innovation of monumental importance. Dry polishing is so much better than the traditional method of washing quinoa to remove the saponin. Washing quinoa uses up precious water resources. It also produces soapy waste water which should be properly disposed of but often isn't. It also requires that the quinoa must be dried after washing, and that uses energy. Dry polishing is the only way to go.

These days, many quinoa processors, and almost all those in Bolivia, use a combination of dry polishing (also called scarification), washing and drying. Many still use only the washing and drying method. This is unfortunate, as I believe that an experienced rice polisher could replicate what Fontineau did. I expect to one day see some bright engineer come up with a significant technological breakthrough in polishing machine design that would revolutionize quinoa saponin removal. I hope that in the near future all quinoa processors will have precision dry polishers specially for use with quinoa.

Fontineau reported to us that some of the saponin powder he removed from the quinoa blew out the window and landed on some plants. He said those plants grew like crazy! As far as I know, no one has experimented with using saponin in this manner. Who knows what potential benefits this could offer to humanity?

By far the oddest disaster we had with Poblete's quinoa was the shipment of quinoa that had been washed but improperly dried. None of us, in Peru or in the States, noticed that several sacks of quinoa had more than 13% moisture. With that level of moisture, quinoa could mold. The shipment had already been cleaned at Celestial and put into fiber drums and was sitting on our warehouse floor when we realized it had indeed molded. Not only that, in the process of molding it produced some weird substance that burned through the bottom of the drum, and then actually continued to dissolve the concrete floor. *It's eating the damned floor! Oh my God! What kind of monster have we created?* That quinoa had to be carefully disposed of, and the floor repaired. It was all rather bizarre!

Quinoa is Here!

Most of Poblete's quinoa shipments were fine. The quinoa arrived, was packaged and sold, and many thousands of people enjoyed eating it.

Our business and company were growing, but slowly. Financially we were always operating near the edge, getting by one month at a time.

Building distribution and sales turned out to be difficult, far more difficult than we had imagined. After all, nobody had ever heard of quinoa. There was no real demand for it, so we had to bend over backwards to get people interested. We had to be educators as well as businessmen.

Don and I went to individual stores, spoke to managers, gave them quinoa to taste, and gave them samples to give away. Almost always, they liked it and were willing to carry it. But, there was a problem. They didn't want to buy directly from us.

Stores in the natural foods industry buy from distributors, who provide them with catalogs of thousands of products to look at and choose from, send everything they want in one shipment, and present them with one invoice. If the stores bought directly from individual suppliers like us, they would have too many shipments to handle and too many invoices to process.

Since the stores that were interested in carrying quinoa wanted to buy it from their regular distributors, we went to the distributors and did the same presentations, and those people also liked quinoa. But, they too had a problem. They said they couldn't carry it because they didn't have stores ordering it. *What a "Catch 22!"* The way the distribution system worked made it difficult, if not impossible, for people like us to introduce a new product. But, we did it. Slowly.

Don came up with the strategy of selling our quinoa to two of the biggest natural food companies at the time, Eden Foods and Arrowhead Mills. They functioned both as producers as well as distributors. These two companies produced so many different high quality products that stores were willing to buy directly from them.

At first Eden and Arrowhead sold our branded products, but later, upon their request, we supplied them with bulk quinoa to package and sell under their own brand names. Eventually, they found their own supplies of quinoa in South America and cut us out. Our dealings with these two companies served to distribute quinoa but didn't serve our company. Through them, we did get the word out there. We did get more people buying and eating quinoa, but our company didn't benefit.

Natural food companies back in those days were often started by hippies; they were sincere people, totally into natural food, and not particularly interested in just making money for its own sake. I was like that. I wasn't in it for the money. For me business was a tool to accomplish a greater good. Don and I assumed that working with the people in this industry would be a friendly affair. Perhaps our expectations were stuck in the zeitgeist of the 70s. We were looking for brotherly love, but found the opposite. The highly competitive spirit and "me first" attitude of the 80s prevailed.

We found a similar unfriendly attitude among the Arica School administration. They were so intent on bringing money and resources into the school that they forgot the virtue of lending a helping hand to brothers who needed it. We were upset when they tried to cheat us by offering to sell Quinoa Corporation a trademark, "Keenwa," that they didn't own. They had once owned it but had let the registration lapse. We thought we might use it, but then abandoned the idea. We also asked them to send us whatever information they had collected about quinoa, but they declined. It was only through Oscar Ichazo's personal intervention that we got their office files on quinoa transferred to us. As it turned out, it didn't really matter. Although we hoped their files would have something useful in them, they didn't.

Quinoa is here!

Quinoa Corporation never had the money to do everything we needed to do. Not once did we place an ad or commercial for quinoa in magazines, newspapers, TV, or radio. What we did was make banners and little red buttons that simply said "Quinoa is here!"

That's it. That was almost our entire promotional budget. The rest was spent on attending national trade shows.

The first one we showed at was a Natural Foods Expo in Las Vegas, Nevada. Paz and Don's girlfriend, Saskia, came with us and we created the first quinoa salad recipe, based on tabbouli (See Recipe pg. 202). It was a big hit at the show and thereafter. We didn't know enough to pre-arrange for kitchen space to prepare our samples, so the quinoa was made in a rice cooker, and the salad put together in our hotel room. Despite our ineptness, we got food prepared, and it tasted great!

Quinoa was slowly becoming known by more and more people, and we all enjoyed the challenge and excitement of being at trade shows. Unfortunately, we never got enough new orders to offset the expense of appearing at these shows.

The Media Takes Notice of Quinoa

Lacking money for paid advertising, we depended heavily on free media coverage for our quinoa venture. The first newspapers to write stories about quinoa were the local ones, mostly featuring quinoa as a new crop for Colorado.

Later came local articles about quinoa as a food, and finally quinoa got some national attention. We were thrilled by a piece in *The Washington Post*, October 30, 1985: "Laurel's Kitchen rediscovers quinoa, an Incan grain."

An article by Florence Fabricant in *The New York Times* on February 12, 1986, "An Andean legacy, quinoa, arrives here" stated:

"Native to the high Andes of South America, quinoa has been rediscovered as one of the 'heritage' foods that sustained native American populations before the arrival of Europeans.

As such, it joins New Mexican blue corn, the sacred grain of the Hopis used to make silvery paper-thin piki bread, which has successfully made the great leap from the Southwestern reservation to the trendy California kitchen. It's too early to tell if quinoa will catch on in this fashion."

Yes, back in 1986 it was "too early to tell if quinoa will catch on."

The most important, accurate, and complete story was written by Rebecca Wood in the April 1985 issue of the now defunct *East West Journal*. She called it "Quinoa: tale of a food survivor," and declared that, "After centuries of hard times, the nutritious 'mother grain of the Incas' is alive and well in both North and South America."

Rebecca was a highly respected member of the local macrobiotic community, and her article helped spread the word about quinoa to just those people who would be most inclined to use it. The story contained so much factual information that many other articles have been written using her material. Rebecca became a true lover of quinoa and went on to write the first book devoted entirely to quinoa, *Quinoa The Supergrain: Ancient Food for Today*. Rebecca wrote:

> "In a small pot on his office hot plate Gorad brought water to a boil. He added a pinch of salt and some of this new foodstuff. While it simmered, he quietly talked about the politics, history, magic, and mystery of quinoa. By the time it was cooked, my doubts had dissipated. With my first taste, I was hooked."

> "Quinoa is not a new-fangled, low-cal food synthesized from wood chips. It is not a cure-all health-food supplement. Quinoa is more than a nouvelle cuisine experience to titillate jaded palates. Quinoa is a food staple."

National magazines also began writing stories about quinoa. On November 25, 1985, *Newsweek* published "Quinoa: Is one little seed all we need?" *Better Homes and Gardens* featured "Quinoa: Food of the Future: A little seed with big potential" in October 1986. A year later, in October, 1987, quinoa made it to *Food & Wine* magazine in "It's Ancient, It's New, It's Called Quinoa." *Cosmopolitan's* July 1988 issue included an article on quinoa titled "Miracle Grain."

And of course, radio and TV coverage also helped our cause. The Denver NBC affiliate, KCNC-TV, featured quinoa in January 1986; CNN the following month; and in March of that year BBC radio, Voice of America, and NPR all reported on quinoa.

The article that had the greatest impact was the 1985 piece in *Newsweek*. It was a short article with one photo. Jeff Copeland, the author, quoted Duane Johnson, the Colorado State University Professor of Agronomy, as saying:

"If you had your choice of one food to survive on, this would be the best."

FOOD

Quinoa: Is One Little Seed All We Need?

One hundred and fifty years ago bananas were a delicacy virtually unknown in the United States, and peanuts were eaten only by slaves. So who's to say that a seed called quinoa (pronounced keen-wa), eaten by Indians in the Andes, won't be a staple in the American diet by the year 2000? Or the year 1986?

In January quinoa will be distributed nationwide in health-food stores. For about $3, the adventurous consumer can purchase a pound bag of something that looks like canary feed, is cooked like rice and has a squashlike taste with nutty overtones.

Quinoa contains up to 20 percent protein—almost twice that of most grains—and a balance of the essential amino acids, which other grains lack. It is a high-fiber food with no cholesterol that can be used as a meat substitute. "If you had your choice of one food to survive on, this would be the best," says Duane Johnson, an agronomist at Colorado State University, who is trying to develop a strain of the plant that can be cultivated in the

Rocky Mountains. The grain is now laboriously gathered by Indians in the remote Andean villages of Peru, Ecuador, Bolivia and Chile and imported by Don McKinley and Stephen L. Gorad, principals of the Quinoa Corp. in Boulder, Colo.

The two partners plan to introduce the product to the gourmet market at trade shows. If the public bites—and the price drops—quinoa could compete with the last big food-marketing success from the Andes—the potato.

JEFF B. COPELAND in Boulder

JAMES A. COOK—PICTURE GROUP
Grain trust: *Gorad and McKinley stock up*

He ended his article with: "If the public bites—and the price drops—quinoa could compete with the last big food-marketing success from the Andes—the potato."

PROYECTO QUINOA
CASILLA DE CORREO 8
C. P. 5236 VILLA DEL TOTORAL
CORDOBA · PEPUBLICA ARGENTINA

Proyecto Quinoa

Quinoa in Argentina

As hopeful and encouraging as the *Newsweek* article was, what mattered most to me was that it was printed worldwide, including in South America. The article reached the hands of Julio Torres Cabrera in Argentina. Immediately after reading it, Julio wrote to us in his broken English on letterhead from Villa del Totoral, Provincia Córdoba in Argentina. Dated November 30, 1985, it said:

> "Quinoa (Chenopodium quinoa) is a weed that grows freely here in this area, tall about 2 mt, & with a remarcable agressivity against other neighbours. We spend a lot of money in chemical control every year, in other case it would be impossible to make any crop (maize, soy beans, sorghum) to get rid of it. Would you be interested in doing something here in order to transformate this plague in some commercial & exportable crop? Then you can wright to me to..."

I read Julio's letter very carefully. *Wow! Quinoa is growing as an aggressive weed in Argentina!* What a tremendous boon that would have been for us, were it in fact true. I wrote back to Sr. Torres, asking for samples of the seed and photographs of the plant. Julio then mailed back an actual cutting of the plant which included the seeds. Alas, it wasn't quinoa at all. It was lambsquarter, also known as pigweed (Chenopodium album), a common weed cousin of quinoa found all over the world. I wrote and gave him the bad news.

My letter did not stop Julio. He didn't have quinoa growing as a weed on his property, but he had the idea that perhaps he could plant it. Thus began a three-year adventure and a friendship that has lasted until today. Julio looked through church archives in the area and came up with a history of quinoa use in Córdoba dating back centuries. He traveled to the north of Argentina, to Jujuy and Salta where quinoa is still grown, to see what they were doing. He came to Boulder to visit me and

traveled with me in Peru and Bolivia to meet other quinoa people. Julio fell totally in love with quinoa.

I also traveled to Argentina to visit Julio. His style of life was quite different from mine to say the least. Julio enjoyed life to its fullest. I don't know how I survived day after day of successive rounds of champagne drink-

Julio Torres out standing in his field

ing, Cuban cigar smoking, and the *yerba mate* we used to sober up with periodically.

We did a ceremony on his property to ask for the blessings of Incan gods, and Julio planted perhaps more hectares of quinoa in Totoral than he should have. In Argentina everything agricultural is done at a colossal scale.

I flew back to Totoral for the harvest, anticipating driving the combine through beautiful endless fields of mature Argentine quinoa. When I got there it had been raining off and on for over a week. Rain, or even just too much humidity, will cause quinoa to sprout while still in seed heads on the plants. Rain during harvest time is a certain disaster that all quinoa farmers face. Julio's quinoa sprouted and the total crop was ruined. He never planted quinoa again.

Julio Torres, author

When all possibility of doing anything with quinoa, with or without me, failed to materialize, Julio sat himself down and wrote *QuinoaCorp*, an amusing, semi-fictional novel based on his experiences with me and with quinoa.

CHAPTER FOUR

Work and Play in Bolivia

SINCE ALFONSO POBLETE, OUR FIRST supplier, was in Peru, I didn't actually have to go to Bolivia. But I went anyway, and did so many times. From the very beginning I knew I needed to source quinoa in Bolivia, the true motherland of this amazing grain.

On my first trip as an official representative of Quinoa Corporation I was more than a little uneasy. I went to Bolivia to find out the truth of what happened to David Cusack. *Was he killed because of quinoa or was it something else? What was it?* I flew into La Paz and made my first inquiries at the United States Consulate. I learned nothing. I talked with Peter McFarren, the AP reporter who investigated the death. I also visited the Tiahuanaco archeological site where David was shot, looking over my shoulder all the time I was there. I never got a straight story from anyone about David's death. I don't think the people I spoke to knew what had happened or why.

The only thing that became clear to me was that I'd better be extra careful if I didn't want what had happened to David to happen to me. I'm generally careful when I travel to foreign lands, but after David's death I was even more vigilant, at least for the first few trips. I tried to keep a low profile when traveling in Bolivia, and I always kept my eyes wide open for anything that seemed out of the ordinary. Later on, since nothing bad had happened to me, my caution began to feel silly, as there were many other things to do and be concerned about when visiting Bolivia.

The 1985 *Newsweek* article led to the necessity for many trips to Bolivia. All kinds of people who happened to see the article, some serious, many not so serious, wanted to sell me quinoa. I needed to sort through them to find the ones we could actually work with. I did eventually find sincere, reliable contacts, and thus began Quinoa Corporation's practice of importing all of its grain directly from Bolivia, something that has continued through the years.

On my buying trips to South America I usually stayed a month or more. In those days, business success in Latin America depended on relationships, not legalities or contracts, so I spent a lot of time getting to know suppliers and their families. I went to their homes, ate with them, partied with them. It was not at all unpleasant.

Success also depended on my adjustment to their way of doing things, to their rhythms, their timing. Everything in South America, particularly in Bolivia, moved more slowly than in the States, a lot more slowly. I learned that when they agreed to do something, they would do it, but not in a time frame we were used to. The reason for this was quite simple. Getting things done in Bolivia—*anything*—was complicated, difficult, and subject to far more problems than the people back in Boulder realized. I became a sort of translator between two very differ-ent cultures. It was a difficult job, as it is hard for people to truly understand what life is like beyond their own familiar borders.

I also prolonged my trips simply because I enjoyed what I was doing. My visits to South America were exciting, adven-turous, and different, and the people themselves were so very different from what I was used to.

At high altitudes, as on the Bolivian Altiplano, sound trav-els far and with great clarity. On a typical day, the only sounds I heard were people laughing, or talking very softly. Often the only thing I heard was silence. I never heard shouting or angry words. I never saw a fight. The people seemed sort of childlike, and their lives were simple. In a way, the extreme poverty gave these people the sense that they weren't going anywhere. There was nothing to strive for and nothing to fight over. Everything felt rather timeless.

Once I was standing in a crowd of people. There was a woman to my right, and in front of us stood a man, a strang-er to us both. In a sim-ple act of kindness, the woman reached out and quietly picked a piece of lint off the back of his sweater without him even realizing it. There was something about that act that struck me. It was something a child might do, but an adult in my culture would never

Chola in La Paz

think of touching a complete stranger like that; it would be too embarrassing to be caught. Yet, to this *chola* it was a perfectly natural act. To me it seemed sweet.

When I first started buying quinoa, I ran into a most unusual situation regarding pricing. I asked an Aymara woman vendor in the outdoor market how much a kilo of quinoa would cost, and she told me the peso equivalent of fifty cents. But when I asked if I could buy her entire fifty-kilo sack, she said it would cost me the equivalent of $35, or seventy cents per kilo. That didn't seem right to me, so I asked her why it cost more per kilo to buy the whole sack. She answered that if she sells the whole sack to me, she won't have any more to sell. *Hmm*. I found that reasoning rather odd. When I finally met someone who could get me ten such sacks, the price was up to $500, or $1.00/kilo. The more I wanted to buy, the higher the per unit price went. Buying tons of quinoa was going to be costly indeed.

The reason for this perverse inversion of the law of economy of scale was partially that there had never been anyone interested in buying so much quinoa before, and it was going to take extra work to supply what I wanted. That made sense to me. The other reason was the "get it all while you can, because tomorrow may never come" mentality of the Andean peoples. As soon as they realized that I was truly interested in buying their quinoa, they wanted to get as much money as they could from me, right then and there. They weren't interested in mutually beneficial long-term relationships or fair prices. I couldn't blame them. They have always had difficult lives, and bleak, uncertain futures.

In fact, the Aymara have a totally different sense of time than we do. Whereas we look "ahead" to the future and "back" to the past, they see the past in front of them, where they can see it, and the future behind them, where it is hidden. To the Aymara the future is by its very nature totally unknown, and not to be trusted.

One of the odd consequences of this situation was that quinoa, which had lower status than chicken feed in the Andes, immediately became an expensive gourmet food in the United States.

Working in Bolivia was not the same as working in the United States. It was like being on a different planet, one where nothing ever works quite right. What do I mean by that?

During one stay in La Paz, I needed to change an air ticket destination from New York City to Chile, something quite simple in the abstract.

I asked at the hotel reception desk how I might do that, telling them it was a LAN airlines ticket. They looked for the address of the LAN office in their standard hotel directory book, but it wasn't there. So they called information and got a phone number. They called. It was busy, so they gave the number to me to call later.

I went back to my room and called several times. Also busy. When I finally got through, it was a recorded message in Spanish that I didn't understand. So I went back to the lobby to a kiosk that arranges tours, and asked if they could handle flight changes. "No, but the office up in room number 103 can do that." I went there. The door was shut so I knocked, and knocked. No answer. No one in the office. *What do I do now?*

I went out in the street to an area where there seemed to be many tourist offices and walked into the first one, "Coca Tours." The young man there spoke English, and I asked if they could arrange flight changes. "Yes. What airline?" LAN. "No, sorry. You must go there."

"Where is it?"

He looked in his travel agent information book, found an address and wrote down *Edificio 16 de Julio*. I asked him for directions, and he told me to just walk down El Prado, the main street, and I'd find it.

Shoe shine boy

So, I took off down El Prado and soon discovered that there were no building numbers, only names. I had to look at every building for the name *Edificio 16 de Julio*. But of course it might be on the other side of this very wide street, in which case I'd never be able to see the name. After a while I asked a shoe shine boy. They all wear black scarves covering their faces, so you only see their eyes. I don't know why. He told me my building was three blocks down, so I went three blocks down, then four, then five, then several more, and at last there it was, *Edificio 16 de Julio*. I triumphantly entered. I did it! *Hooray!* Deep inside the building was a dimly lit board showing all the tenants and their room numbers. No LAN. I read it over, and over, and then over again. I was quite distraught. No LAN. *What do I do now?*

I started walking back up El Prado, up also meaning uphill, and saw another travel agency with a big sign in the window "WE SPEAK ENGLISH." I entered and asked, "Do you speak English?" I thought it would be a lot easier explaining my dire situation in English. The first person said "No," as did the remaining four people in the office. *O.K., no English spoken here.*

So, I sat across from a kindly looking lady and told her my tale in Spanish. She said emphatically that I would have to go to the LAN office to change my ticket, and that it was in the Zona Sur.

La Paz is built into an immense downward sloping hole in the Altiplano. The rich people live near the bottom in the south because there is more oxygen in the air, and it is warmer. My hotel was in the higher altitude north. I was staying at the Hotel Gloria, which I booked only because they advertised a vegetarian restaurant, which in fact did not exist. Zona Sur was a good hour away, considering that there is always a traffic jam in La Paz. I asked about what time they closed. "Three." O.K., it looked like I would have enough time if I got right on it. I asked her to write the address down. She handed me a piece of scrap paper with *Calle 21 San Miguel* on it.

I rushed outside to find a taxi. Then I realized that I didn't know how to recognize a taxi here. So I stood in the heavily congested street at grave risk to my life and sort of waved an arm. An ordinary car stopped, so I got in and handed the driver the paper with the address. He said "No," and waved me out of his cab. Oh, I thought maybe not all cabs want to go all the way to the south. So I tried another, this time asking through the window. "No." This was repeated six times. *What do I do now?* The clock was ticking. What else could I do but try yet another taxi. Finally one driver said he would take me.

About an hour later we arrived at *Calle 21* in the area called *San Miguel*. I took the paper back from the driver and realized that she didn't write down an address, just a street name. No building number or name. We drove down the whole street looking, he and I, for some sign of LAN. We drove the entire length of the street, and then back up, and then down again. We stopped and asked someone. "No." The clock was ticking.

Finally I noticed something that looked like a travel agency with a small LAN sign in the window. *Oh, that must be it. Please!* The cab stopped, I rushed out, and asked him to wait for me. I walked inside, thinking I was at the end of my odyssey. I asked if I could change a LAN flight there. After some confusion the owner explained that I could only do that at a LAN office. "Isn't this it?" I asked. "No." He went outside and told the cab driver where to go. I thanked him profusely, and we took off down some other street. We couldn't see any LAN sign, but I urged the driver to continue.

There, at the end of the street was LAN!!! It was just before three o'clock. I went in and changed my ticket, and had to pay a hefty penalty. It had taken a lot of time and effort, with way too many obstacles and pitfalls, but eventually I did accomplish my goal. It was done!

Before entering the LAN office I'd asked the taxi driver to wait for me, so I could get back up to my hotel. When I finished and walked out of the office, I looked for him. He was gone! Yes, yet another problem. I'd have to look for another taxi to take me back.

Just another typical day in Bolivia!

During another trip I had the bad luck of getting caught in a revolution. I was in La Paz. I'd finished my work and was looking forward to going back home. It was not to be. The airport had been blockaded by some sort of worker group and I couldn't leave. The news broadcasts said that La Paz was completely surrounded and food was about to get scarce. Everyone around me was anxious. They didn't know what was going to happen next. All gas stations in the area were under rebel control, which made travel over land impossible. Although La Paz itself was relatively quiet, there were reports of gunfire up in El Alto and the surrounding countryside.

What was I to do?

My Bolivian associates proposed putting me in a minivan with a big drum full of gasoline, and driving me to the border with Peru. The thought of sharing the passenger compartment of a minivan with a drum of gasoline while bullets are flying made me more than a little nervous. I went anyway. What else could I do? I made it to Peru without incident and gratefully flew home.

I don't think the people in Boulder ever truly understood what I had to go through on my buying trips.

On several occasions Paz accompanied me to Bolivia. On one such trip Oscar Ichazo's daughter, Carolina, and her Canadian husband, Michael, invited us to drive with them down from the Altiplano to a lower and more comfortable elevation. We were going to Coroico, a small village in the Yungas region, an area about a thousand feet above Bolivia's Amazon jungle, but about ten thousand feet lower than the Altiplano. Incidentally, the Yungas is where all the coca is grown.

The day started out calmly, full of expectations of tropical warmth and better oxygenated air. Little did I know they were taking us down the notorious Yungas Road, also known as the "Death Road," or what the Inter-American Development Bank christened the "world's most dangerous road." We left early in the morning, passing through a barren stretch of roadway populated by stray dogs, dozens of them, waiting by the side of the road for sympathetic travelers to toss scraps of food from their car windows. We gave the dogs whatever we could and proceeded on until Michael's car began to overheat. Fortunately we were near a small town.

It turned out to be something simple, a broken fan belt, but finding a replacement part and someone to do the work in

The Yungas Road

this rustic town took us the better part of the day. We had lunch and sat around biding our time until the car was ready to go. I'd never heard of the Yungas Road and didn't understand why Michael and Carolina debated the decision to go on or return home so intensely. *So what if we drive while it's dark?*, I thought. Michael decided we should continue, so we did.

Then we entered the "Road." Immediately I saw what all the concern was about. The damned road was cut into the side of a cliff. To our left was a wall of earth. To our right the cliff fell off into what looked like a bottomless pit, a drop of several thousand feet, with jungle below. There was no guardrail, no posts, no nothing. What made matters worse was that the road itself was unpaved — just dirt — and full of rocks and holes. And worse than that, it was narrow, in many places only wide enough for one car. I couldn't believe it.

Could it get any worse? Yes!

As we proceeded down the road, we found ourselves enshrouded first by fog, and a little later, darkness and fog. The headlights were useless, as they just lit up the fog. We couldn't see two feet in front of the car. We literally inched along that road. I could have walked faster. Michael kept the car far over to the left, feeling for the wall with his outstretched left hand. He did not move forward unless his hand was touching the wall. This was the only way to guarantee that we wouldn't inadvertently drift off to the right side of the road and down to our certain deaths.

I sat in the back feeling totally powerless. I couldn't believe what we had gotten ourselves into. *Why, oh why, are we doing this?*, I kept thinking. But by that point I could only sit there on the edge of my seat and watch. Watch I did, with all the attention I could muster. But watch what? There was nothing to see but fog.

Nobody in the car dared speak a word. I'm not sure if anyone was even breathing.

Then we heard screaming. *"Socorro, socorro!"* (Help, help!) Yes, in the middle of our nightmare, we drove right into someone else's far worse nightmare. A car heading in the same direction had gone over the cliff with four people inside. Thank God, the car was right there in sight; it had miraculously fallen into some small trees just off the cliff. We stopped and helped a man, his wife and child, and the wife's mother all climb back up to the road. The women were hysterical, the child frightened and crying, and the man very concerned about his car and the belongings in it. It took over an hour to get everyone up and calmed down. They had been going to the jungle on a vacation.

During that time several cars passed slowly by, but sadly no one else stopped to help. I learned that Bolivians in those times considered it dangerous to stop and help people in distress. It might be a trick that robbers use.

We packed the two women and child into our car and continued on. The man chose to stay with his car, as he was afraid it or the belongings in it would be stolen by the time he could get back to it. It seemed strange to me, but perhaps he was right.

We succeeded in getting to Coroico early that morning, made sure the family was taken care of, and then spent a pleasant day eating, drinking, and relaxing in the sweet warmth and oxygen-rich air of the Yungas. It felt good to still be alive.

Not all my trips to Bolivia involved difficulties or danger. Some were just funny, quirky even. On one such trip with Paz, we entered into a sort of economic fantasy world. The year was 1985 and Bolivia was in one of the worst periods of hyper-inflation that the world had ever seen. The one million peso note was only worth fifty cents. The Bolivian peso had depreciated roughly 40,000 percent, sometimes losing one to two percent of its value per hour.

As inflation raged and the peso lost value, prices rose. The government needed to keep printing and circulating bills of larger and larger denomination, a feat

5,000,000 peso bill

they couldn't quite manage. Instead, people made bundles out of identical bills and tied them together with string. Everyone accepted that let's say a five-inch stack of thousand-peso bills was equivalent to a cup of coffee, or a ten-inch-high stack of ten-thousand-peso bills could buy you a chicken. People paid for everything with measured bundles of bills. Nobody ever actually counted the number of bills in a bunch; they just measured them, or if the value was in fact critical, they would weigh the bundle. All around La Paz you would see people carrying shopping bags full of bundled bills. It was totally surreal.

As a gringo visiting Bolivia with U.S. dollars in his pocket, I felt magically transformed into one of the richest men in the world. My meager dollar was worth a fortune. I could buy anything I wanted, and not think twice about the price. But I was in Bolivia; honestly, what was there to buy? Furthermore, I did not want to abuse this artificially created situation. Nevertheless, I did take Paz, Carolina and Michael out to one of the fanciest restaurants in La Paz. The four of us ate a wonderful meal, complete with wine and desserts, and the bill came to—sorry, you aren't going to believe this—fifteen cents!!!

I would never again be as rich as this for the rest of my life.

A Very Strange Tale

The first letter I got from Miguel Jorge Seoane Carvajal, an administrator at the local Santa Cruz branch of the Banco Central de Bolivia, was dated August 8, 1985. Seoane wrote that he had several irregular ball-shaped pieces of a hardened dough-like substance, the largest about the size of a softball, that had been dug up in the jungle sixteen years ago. Laboratory analysis, he claimed, revealed that they were over 2,500 years old and that these balls were made out of quinoa.

Despite such formidable antiquity, this quinoa was still quite edible, he reported, and in fact, he had prepared and enjoyed a delicious soup made from a piece of this perfectly preserved quinoa. Seoane further suggested that the origin of these balls was Incan. He also took the trouble to assure me, in no uncertain terms, that he was a serious person and that all he was telling me was real and true.

During the following months we exchanged a series of friendly letters. I asked a lot of questions and Seoane answered

with little bits and pieces of information. I told him that my early training had grounded me in science, and that I had a rather
hard-headed, skeptical outlook. But, I explained, later experiences with spiritual masters, along with seemingly miraculous
healings and other mysteries of that nature, had opened my
mind to subjects as unusual as his. I thought myself a perfect,
though somewhat reluctant, recipient for his discovery, and he
readily agreed.

Seoane was looking for a partner who could do the necessary investigations to determine exactly how this quinoa managed to survive the ravages of time. The process of preservation
needed to be discovered and then reproduced. He was sure
that this would be of tremendous value to humanity, and that
humanity would be willing to pay handsomely for its secrets.
He generously offered to share all future economic benefit from
this project with me.

Seoane asked me to come visit him. He wanted to show me
these balls of ancient quinoa, and talk about what to do about
them. I was curious, damned curious!

I began by researching the literature on preservation of
organic materials. I read some interesting papers about human
bodies found in Scottish bogs and about "mummy" seeds found
in ancient jars. There was a recent case of some 2,300-year-old
seeds discovered in a well-preserved condition under water in
a spring in Italy by Prof. J.C. Carter, an archeologist at the University of Texas. I contacted him. He sent me to Vivien Toole at
the United States Department of Agriculture who informed me
that the common belief that ancient or "mummy" seeds could
still be alive is totally false. I learned something interesting, but
it wasn't anything that shed light on Seoane's quinoa find. My

readings, however, led me to consider and propose that the quinoa balls might not have been intentionally preserved, but rather that they were maintained by some unusual natural process. Seoane thought my suggestion was ridiculous.

My research did not disprove the possibility of 2,500-year-old balls of still edible quinoa; so, although I was skeptical, I also maintained an open mind about them. I continued trading letters with my new Bolivian acquaintance until it was time for another quinoa buying trip. My buying always took place in La Paz or in other towns on the Altiplano. This time I scheduled a side trip down to Santa Cruz in the jungle.

Although it was a relief to get out of the oxygen-poor air of La Paz, the Bolivian jungle was no paradise either. It was hot, wet, and buggy, and everything seemed to move very, very slowly. I took a typical beat-up, tropical zone taxi to Seoane's house on September 18, 1986. The roads were of course dirt, with lots of holes to weave around at top speed, and mangy, flea-bitten dogs to avoid hitting. It was just what one might expect.

The house, though in a poor neighborhood, was larger than I expected. I was invited in and placed at the dining room table. It struck me as odd that there was almost no furniture in the house, just very bare essentials. Miguel Seoane brought out the obligatory bottle of local alcohol, perhaps *aguardiente*, and two small glasses. Out of the corner of my eye I saw his three small children sneaking a glimpse of the strange gringo, and once I saw his wife pass by the doorway, but they were not part of the main action in this scene. His old rifle, on the other hand, was clearly important. Seoane laid it on the table ceremoniously and I was asked to inspect it.

There was an edgy, almost violent atmosphere hanging in the air, mixed in equal measure with the quiet desperation one finds in places of poverty. Add to this the strangeness of a Bolivian jungle town, and more than a bit of alcohol, and you have a particularly disquieting cocktail. There was nothing directly threatening about Seoane, but I was definitely not my usual relaxed self.

Soon after we started drinking, he began telling me his strange tale. He told me that as a young man he and his father had seen a flying saucer right over their heads while they were deep in the jungles of Beni. It had flown low, and he could clearly make out the markings on the belly of the craft. He had tried to tell people about his experience, and of course they just thought he was crazy. But he knew what he saw, and he knew it was real. He remembered the markings and had them engraved on a ring, which he'd worn ever since. I examined the ring on his finger, and after asking permission, I carefully copied the markings onto a piece of paper.

Then he brought out the balls of ancient quinoa. He told me that he believed that extraterrestrials, which he knew existed, had taught the Inca soldiers a method for preserving foodstuffs unknown on our planet. The Inca were highland dwelling peoples, but they often sent soldiers down to conquer and then patrol the jungle tribes. Up on the Altiplano, where quinoa was grown, they built storehouses of grain to feed their armies. Down in the jungle, Seoane conjectured, the Inca made a dough out of the quinoa, formed it into balls, applied the preservation technique taught to them by their outer space brothers, and buried the balls beneath the jungle floor. The Inca armies lived on this.

Seoane said the balls were between 2,500 and 10,000 years old. I recognized that this didn't coincide with the period of the Inca civilization; but I just assumed that he wasn't good with dates, particularly when drunk. The balls were found in the vicinity of the river *Madre de Dios* (Mother of God) near the town of Riberalta. He told me that others were found near three rivers whose translated names were "Hand of God," "Four Hands," and "Divine Hand." The balls, which he called *masa* (dough balls) had been three times their present size when fresh, and had the consistency of badly cooked cake. Some were as large as twenty-four kilograms in weight when fresh, although most were much smaller.

Some were found near the surface, due to soil erosion, and others were buried as deep as two meters. All of them were in a "wet" state when they were just found, and none seemed to have been disturbed or eaten by animals. The local indigenous people, however, ate them when they could find one, and called them *Pan de Indio* (Indian bread).

Miguel Seoane then took a pocketknife from his trousers, scraped off some shavings from one of the balls, and put it in some water to rehydrate. He insisted that I eat it. Reluctantly, I did as he asked. It wasn't so bad. Really! It tasted a bit like stale rye bread. I was already quite drunk, so it was no big deal! I've certainly eaten worse.

Once I was introduced to the balls, the conversation turned to business. Miguel was sure that the preservation technique was worth millions, perhaps billions. After all, these balls of quinoa had survived the usual jungle decay for over 2,500 years. Could you imagine burying a loaf of bread in the jungle and then going to look for it two days later? You know for sure that you wouldn't find anything remotely resembling bread!

Much to my surprise, Seoane entrusted to me several of the balls. He wanted me to take them back to the States and find out the secret of their pres-

Ball of ancient quinoa

ervation. Then we would split the millions we would make fifty-fifty.

He ushered me out the door and back into a taxi. I kept my precious cargo close to me as I rode back to the hotel. I stared at them in my room. I couldn't quite believe what had fallen into my hands. I didn't know for sure what exactly I had, but if even a little bit of his story was true, the possibilities would be enormous. Days passed as I completed my regular business in La Paz, and I eventually caught a plane back to the States.

I worried a lot about crossing U.S. Customs in Miami. Because I often had many different kinds and colors of quinoa seeds, giant or purple corn, Andean potatoes, *tarwi*, or some other exotica with me, I was almost always stopped in Miami when returning from South America. I had the proper license to make it all legal, but the inspectors had to look at everything anyway. This time I had these strange-looking balls of alien preserved Inca quinoa that were going to revolutionize food storage on planet Earth. *What do I say if they ask me, "What is this?" Yeah, very funny!* To my eyes these balls seemed to actually glow with an unmistakable aura of greatness. They certainly didn't look like anything anyone had ever seen before. Surely there was something "alien" about them, but to the customs inspectors they were just more junk in the bag of someone who obviously likes to collect weird junk. They barely noticed them.

I made it back to my office in Boulder. *Now what do I do?* Miguel Seoane warned me that once people knew what I had, they would try to steal the secret. Somehow I had to manage the investigation so that no one knew all the facts. I must never give an intact ball to anyone. It was clear that if they had a ball, they would also have access to the secrets it contained. *Where do I start?* Well, one element was easy for me to check.

I showed my drawing of the flying saucer markings to Paz's brother, Tono Huneeus, a journalist who reported on UFO phenomena. He had been collecting, cataloging, and critiquing sightings for many years. My drawing checked out one hundred percent. The very same markings were sighted on the belly of a presumed flying saucer that was said to have flown over Madrid, Spain in June of 1967, and it was reproduced in a book of such markings. One element of the story was confirmed! *Excellent!*

The fact that I now thought that Seoane's quinoa balls might actually be what he believed them to be led me to be extremely

My original drawing

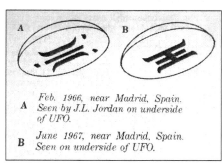

A   Feb. 1966, near Madrid, Spain. Seen by J.L. Jordan on underside of UFO.

B   June 1967, near Madrid, Spain. Seen on underside of UFO.

Markings reproduced in a UFO book

cautious, perhaps even to the point of paranoia. I couldn't tell the whole story to anyone. They would never believe me. *Never!* But if they did, they would certainly try to steal the secret. I was also held back by a nagging doubt as to whether human scientists could ever discover and replicate a preservation technique that may have had its origins in another galaxy. I moved slowly, hesitantly.

My next significant step didn't occur until July of 1987, when I sent a small piece of one of the balls to Beta Analytic Inc., in Coral Gables, Florida, one of the few places that did carbon dating. I received back some disconcerting news.

You must realize that my new friend, Miguel Seoane, was a sincere man working in a bank at a boring, bureaucratic and poorly paying job. He had a nice family, perhaps a drinking problem, a love of guns, and not much else. These balls of quinoa were his dream. There was no other way he was going to escape from the poverty of his existence. The secret that lay inside these few quinoa chunks meant everything to him. But his dream started to unravel in my hands.

The date came back as 260 BP, which translates to the calendar year 1690 with an error range of plus or minus sixty years. This didn't make any sense at all. It is well after the demise of the Inca Empire, and too old to be a modern fake. *What is this?*

I then told pieces of my story to a friend who worked at the Harvard University Museum of Comparative Zoology. He in turn passed bits of the story on to Dr. Jean Boise of the Farlow Reference Library and Herbarium of Cryptogamic Botany, also part of Harvard University. Dr. Boise expressed a tentative opinion that my great balls of quinoa might perhaps be a fungus.

Now I was puzzled, and I wrote back to Seoane on September 11, 1987, with grave doubt ringing in my words. "Why did you tell me that it is 2,000-year-old quinoa? On what basis do you know this to be true? Do you have the laboratory reports? If you do, please send me copies."

Seoane replied to the suggestion that what we had was some sort of fungus with ". . . *nada es mas ridiculo*" (nothing could be more ridiculous). He reiterated that what we had was real and of enormous importance. He informed me that the analyses were done at the *Instituto de Investigaciones de Tiwanako*, but that he didn't have the papers to send me.

The more questions I asked him, the more suspicious he became of me. He didn't doubt his discovery; he doubted me. He started thinking that I was trying to steal the whole thing for myself. I didn't know what to do. If his dream was true, I had the responsibility to protect it. If not, I would be breaking this poor man. I knew that ultimately I had to be on the side of truth, no matter what the consequences were for him or me.

I decided I had to come fully out in the open with what I had, so I sent an intact ball to Dr. Boise at Harvard University for thorough analysis. I diplomatically neglected to mention the part about extraterrestrials. On November 6, 1987 I got a letter that stated:

> "Microscopic inspection revealed the cellular structure of the item to be filamentous and exhibiting no blueing in the presence of iodine (no starch present). These findings indicate that the Bolivian collection is not plant in origin but a fungus. By my assessment, it is likely that it is a sclerotium (resting body) of a species of Polyporus . . . ."

Fungus!!! The stupid thing is some kind of mushroom. No wonder it was under the dirt of the jungle floor. And I ate the damned thing!

When I wrote Miguel Seoane with this definitive information, he became extremely displeased with me. Now he was sure that I was trying to steal his fortune. In response, I mailed him a xerox copy of an article sent to me by Dr. Boise that appeared in *Mycologia* 11: 104 in 1919, by H.T. Gussow

Canadian Tuckahoe photo

entitled "The Canadian Tuckahoe." In it was a reference to an 1881 article that cited the existence of this fungus in jungles and the fact that it is sometimes called *Pan de Indio.* The article also contained excellent photographs. They showed objects that were indisputably the same as the balls of "quinoa" I had on my desk.

Miguel Seoane never wrote back. I do not know what happened with him or whether he managed to move on from his shattered dream. I sent most of the remaining balls to Dr. Boise. Harvard was happy to have these rare specimens in their collection, and I still have one to remind me of my strange adventure in the land of dreams, hope, and illusion.

CHAPTER FIVE

A Million Dollars from Down Under

BACK IN BOULDER, QUINOA CORPORATION was struggling every day to make ends meet. Introducing a totally unknown food into the U.S. market was never going to be an easy task. We knew what we had to do, but we didn't have the money to do it.

Then, one fine day, Don met Sam Simpson at a social gathering in Denver. Sam was a tall, good-looking, well-dressed, and polite young man, and Don was naturally attracted to talking with him. In the course of their conversations Don brought up the fact that he was doing business with a very interesting new food and that we were in need of capital for expansion.

Sam in turn explained to Don that he was president of Great Eastern International Inc. (GEII), an Australian owned shell company registered as a publicly traded corporation in the United States. He told Don that Great Eastern had no active business at the time and was looking to build a portfolio of acquisitions. Sam was their man in the U.S., and it was his job to find the right companies to buy.

That fateful conversation led to further informal meetings and eventually to business negotiations. Sam spoke with Brian Frost, his boss in Australia, the one who made all the big decisions. Don introduced me to Sam, and I, of course, talked on and on about quinoa and about how unbelievably great it is. At one point, after several days of listening to me, Sam confided in Don that he was concerned that we might be some sort of cult.

Neither Sam nor Brian thought that much about quinoa itself. Their tastes tended more toward meat and potatoes. But they did come to believe that quinoa's story was unusual and exciting, and that it might drum up interest and add value to their company. They talked about "selling the sizzle and not the steak," a phrase originated by the legendary salesman and motivational speaker Elmer Wheeler in the 1930's that refers to marketing the excitement for a product instead of the product itself. Quinoa, or rather the story of quinoa, looked to them like it could be a money maker. Brian flew to Boulder, and amidst the cloud of his ever present cigar smoke, offered us a deal.

Great Eastern was willing to invest a million dollars in Quinoa Corporation. They would own 100% of the company, and in turn Don and I would be issued stock in GEII, be given employment contracts at $60,000/year, and receive a one time signing bonus of $30,000 each. I would remain as CEO and president, and Don would become vice president in charge of sales and marketing.

Don loved the deal.

I didn't.

I looked at it, why it was being offered, and who was offering it, and it just didn't feel right to me. The terms and the money were fine. That wasn't the problem.

I thought about how difficult the road had been for quinoa and for us since the very beginning. We'd weathered crisis after crisis, and stood on the brink of disaster more times than we could count. David's death was an unbelievably great tragedy, but it was just one of many almost catastrophic events in our history. And yet somehow we managed to survive. Something always happened, usually at the very last minute, not only to save us, but to keep us moving forward.

I felt certain that it wasn't our skill at business that had kept us afloat. We just weren't that experienced or knowledgeable about what we were doing. It had to be something else. I thought of that something else as "grace," and I believed that we received grace because we were selflessly doing what had to be done. We were on a mission for quinoa, in a sense masquerading as a business. We fully recognized quinoa's unique goodness and her importance, and were serious about getting quinoa known and used throughout the world. We worked for quinoa. We were not doing it for the money, at least I wasn't.

My feelings about the difference between our mission and ordinary business had been clarified some months earlier when I attended a one-day seminar put on by the M.I.T. management school. I went thinking I might absorb something useful from real business professionals. What I learned was that the true purpose, the goal, the motivation for running a company was to make money, and that it didn't matter how one made that money. The product itself didn't matter! The quality of the product wasn't important as long as it sold well. The theory was that faulty or detrimental products would get weeded out eventually by market forces. I couldn't believe what I had heard. I left that seminar feeling like I had just met the devil himself.

It was clear to me that Great Eastern was a business run by businessmen, and they were only interested in making money.

Don and I met in the kitchen at Quinoa Corporation and talked.

"Don, up until now this company has stayed alive only through grace. We've survived despite our lack of skills. If we take this deal, we'll have to run it like any ordinary business, and we'll have to be really, really good at what we do. The grace won't be there any more to save our sorry asses."

Don got angry. In his eyes this was the deal of a lifetime, being offered at a time when we truly needed it. He thought my words were spiritual mumbo jumbo. He thought me naive, impractical, and out of reality. Perhaps he was right. And then again, perhaps he wasn't.

I saw how important this deal was to Don, and I didn't have any alternative to offer except to continue as before, always on the edge of disaster. I wasn't sure we could go on living like that much longer, so I bowed to the pressures of the situation and said "O.K." I also made the commitment that once I agreed to do this, I would put one hundred percent of my effort into running Quinoa Corporation as a real business, a business like all businesses, one designed to make money. If this was going to be the next step in quinoa's journey out of obscurity, so be it. I would try as hard as I could to make it work.

After we closed the deal with Great Eastern on February 28, 1986 nothing was ever the same again. The next two years brought changes to all aspects of our business. It quickly became obvious that our new owners wanted everything done by the book. Sam was a lawyer, so every action we took had to be justified in detail and backed up with a legally binding piece of paper.

With money in the bank, we expanded our office and warehouse space. We bought and installed our own cleaning machinery, including screen separators, a gravity table, grain elevators that went up to the ceiling, and huge storage bins. It was a massive project. We were finally self sufficient when it came to cleaning container-loads of incoming quinoa. We finally had a way to fill twenty-five pound bags auto-

Don in our new warehouse

matically. We had a noisy and very, very dusty factory running in our back room.

We went on a hiring spree. Great Eastern required us to have an in-house bookkeeper. We also hired a new reception-ist, an office assistant, and a person to manage the back room. Great Eastern put their own CPA, Dennis Johanningmeier, in our office. Although they never openly acknowledged that this was his function, we knew what he was. Dennis was their spy. Nevertheless, I fully enjoyed his always smiling and genuinely friendly presence.

The most significant and far-reaching addition to our team was David Schnorr. Dave lived in Los Angeles and had worked in sales for one of the big natural food companies of that era, the Hain Pure Food Company. As he was driving home from work in March 1986 listening to the radio, he heard the interview with me on NPR. He became fascinated with quinoa and even tried to buy some, but couldn't find any. Later that same year, Hain was sold to Pet, Inc. and Dave, along with many others, was out of a job.

Dave saw and answered an inconspicuous, three-line help wanted ad we had placed in the *L.A. Times*. When Dennis called him on behalf of Quinoa Corporation, Dave remembered the NPR interview and the quinoa story, and he knew instantly that he wanted to work for us. He wanted something "worthwhile" to do with his life, not just another high paying sales job; so on April Fools Day, 1987 he became our national sales manager. Little did Dave know how that decision would change his life forever.

David Schnorr was a professional with excellent contacts within the industry, and he knew exactly how to get products into distribution. Although he cautioned us that this was going to be a "long, hard, slow process," we managed to go from selling 65,000 pounds of quinoa in all of 1985 to 65,000 pounds per month by the end of 1987, his first year on the job.

Don and I felt a responsibility to Dave that we didn't have toward ourselves or each other. He was married, had children to raise, and had a house and car to pay off. Don and I were used to crazy risk taking. David deserved stability. He had responsibilities, and we were concerned about taking care of him. As it turned out, with his salary and commissions, Dave earned more money than Don or I, although it was less than what he was used to.

The 80s were a strange time in business, when takeovers and arbitrage deals made headlines daily. We were not entirely exempt from such activity. One day, quite out of the blue, someone with a heavy Australian accent showed up in Boulder and stunned us with "Hi, I'm your new boss!" Apparently there had been a power play back in Australia over control of Great Eastern, and Brian Frost had lost out to this person. He didn't last long however; Brian was soon back in control and we never heard from this other guy again.

Our new "Ancient Harvest" brand with "Supergrain of the Future" trademarked

Although we owned the name Quinoa Corporation and had trademarked the phrase "Supergrain of the Future," Don realized that we had never created a registered brand name for our products. I was on one of my many long trips to South America when a brand name was decided on, and if truth be told, had I been in Boulder I never would have agreed to that brand name. "Ancient Harvest" just didn't sound that appealing to me. Maybe it was a good thing I was away; the "Ancient Harvest" brand has endured all these years, and more recently other companies have joined in on the ancient grains marketing bandwagon.

Along with our new brand name came new products, including quinoa-based pasta and a complete redesign of our packaging and promotional material. We expanded our presence at the Natural Foods Expo and at shows for specialty and gourmet foods. To our credit, by the beginning of 1988 we had nationwide distribution in most natural food stores, in some specialty and gourmet stores, and even in a few forward thinking supermarkets.

Dave, Don, and Gloria at the Natural Foods Expo

Although all of this new equipment, expansion of activities, and hiring sounds like everything was great, it wasn't. All of this, of course, cost money. We were quickly running through the million dollars Great Eastern put into our operation. Given the investments we made in infrastructure and marketing, we needed revenues to increase accordingly, but they didn't. Sales weren't moving as we had hoped.

The Slide Downward

After the international edition of the *Newsweek* article appeared, Bolivians contacted me wanting to sell us quinoa. Among the many hopefuls, one company, BOINSA, stood out in terms of sophistication in dealing with the logistics of export, and eventually I chose them as our first Bolivian supplier.

I was down in Bolivia meeting with them when they put an offer of ten container-loads (about two hundred metric tons) on the table at a reasonable price. It was like a dream come true. But do we need all this quinoa at this time? I phoned back to Boulder to discuss whether I should buy such a huge amount. Brian Frost was there, with Sam and Don.

For many months we had all been discussing why sales were moving so slowly, and what we should do about it. Don's position was that he couldn't move more aggressively on sales unless we had the supply to back him up. He maintained that, as a fundamental law of business, one must never run out of supply once sales were happening, and that doing so would be nothing short of disaster. Don was adamant about this. I didn't know what to think, but I took him at his word.

I reasoned that if I contracted for all that quinoa, Don might feel more secure about having enough supply. Without supply worries, perhaps he could sell with greater confidence. Maybe buying BOINSA's ten containers would be the key we needed for opening the door to more sales.

But I couldn't make that call. Brian Frost was the one who had to make the final decision. His response was, "Look, we never actually tested the waters with quinoa in a big way. Let's buy it all and see if we can sell it." So, I bought the ten containers of quinoa. It was a huge positive step for us as a company. But it was also a gamble. Why? Because by so doing, we tied up over $200,000 of our already rapidly dwindling pool of capital.

Months passed by, the containers of quinoa flowed into our warehouse, and there was no big jump in sales. Nothing much changed. All those dollars sat in inventory, sales continued to grow ever so slowly, and the inevitable happened ... we found ourselves running out of money.

Strangely, my unusual success at finding supply may have led to the demise of our business.

During this period, tensions in the office crept ever upwards. People can feel in their guts that a business is failing. Everyone was anxious, but no one knew what to do. The mood turned glum. All we had was blind hope. A turn-around was always possible; some new publicity, perhaps a deal with a supermarket chain, or something totally unknown could have changed

Don wasn't happy

our fortunes at any moment. But it didn't happen that way.

As our situation worsened Don seemed increasingly withdrawn and moody. It became harder for us to talk about anything. These were not happy times. Don believed in his strategy and insisted on working only with Dave Schnorr. One of our employees came into my office and asked if he should get on the phone, talk to people, and somehow drum up some new sales. He pleaded with me, "Surely there must be something we can do." I had to say "No. Sales are Don's exclusive territory."

I could see that Don and Dave as a team made all the right technical moves when it came to sales, but I also thought that there was something missing. Don's expertise was in marketing, how to present a product, how things should look, and he did that well. But was he the right person to handle sales? Aren't sales people supposed to be out-going, overly friendly, perhaps even aggressive? Don wasn't that type of person.

Although I was CEO of the company, it was a title that carried little weight when it came to my relationship with Don. In reality we were still equal partners, just as we had been from the beginning. My expertise was about quinoa and about finding supply. I knew little about running a company, particularly one in crisis. I knew even less about how to manage the roles of good friend and corporate officer when they came into conflict.

Perhaps a real CEO would have stepped in and taken over the job of sales, or hired someone else to do it.

And perhaps it wouldn't have made any difference at all. Perhaps the world just wasn't ready for quinoa at that time. Hindsight would suggest that this was indeed the case.

What did happen was that Quinoa Corporation slowly slid downhill toward an ever-widening abyss. We laid people off. Several were fired by Dennis while I was out of the country. We rented out office space. We cut people's hours. Don and I took 50% pay cuts in February of 1988, as did Dave a bit later. While this was happening, Great Eastern lost confidence in us and refused to put more money into the company. Instead they made it known that they were willing to sell Quinoa Corporation for any reasonable offer.

A company in Oakland, California, RAM Group, expressed an interest. Kevin McCullough, our board member with the Harvard MBA, and I flew out there to talk with them. They had done their due diligence on quinoa and thought it could be a good business for them. They were interested in buying our company. RAM Group recognized that they needed me for supply, so they told us they wanted me to stay. But they also said they had their own in-house sales and marketing team, so they didn't want Don.

I honestly didn't know what to do. Don and I had gone through hell together building this company up from scratch. How could I go on without him? In many respects I felt like the business belonged to him more than to me. My love was quinoa; his was the business. We had started out as best friends, always watching each other's back. I couldn't accept the RAM Group offer without betraying our friendship.

I turned to Kevin for advice, and he said firmly that as CEO my decision had to be in the best interests of the company. I thought it would be irresponsible to turn down the only chance we had to save Quinoa Corporation, so I told RAM Group that I was interested and communicated that to Dennis and Sam. Then, for reasons unknown to us, RAM Group withdrew their offer.

Don never said anything about any of this to me, but of course he knew what I had done and must have seen it as a signal that our friendship was over and we had parted ways.

Julio Torres, my Argentine friend, was the only other person I knew who was trying to buy Quinoa Corporation from Great Eastern. At one point he got Bunge Born, an Argentine mega-company, one of the world's biggest grain and oilseed traders, interested in us. Being owned by one of the giants of grain trade would have been an enormous step up for quinoa, and for us. The prospects of a deal with them were more than exciting, but nothing came of it. Given the state of financial markets at the time, they calculated that they could make more money with less risk by collecting interest than by making investments.

Julio also did his best to keep me sane in those times of grave difficulty, mostly with his sense of humor. His letters were peppered with comments such as, "Dear friend, if you fail fighting, you failed, OK; but if you quit I go to the States and cut your stones with a rusty tin can edge." (December 1987). A month later, when things were even worse, he wrote, "This is only a game, bloody old chap, cross your fingers and pray to your gods."

CHAPTER SIX

Headaches

THE SHOOTING DEATH OF DAVID CUSACK in 1984 abruptly thrust into my hands the job of finding quinoa supply in South America. It required that I follow in David's footsteps and travel back and forth to Bolivia, despite the possibilities of danger. I did what I had to do. Nothing bad happened to me, or so I thought. You see, the danger confronting me wasn't obvious like getting shot to death, or falling off a cliff. It was far more subtle and quite insidious.

I began getting headaches.

At first I didn't think much about it, as just about everyone gets headaches. But then they became more and more frequent, until one day I realized they had become a permanent part of my everyday existence.

The headaches were not the blindingly intense migraine or the so-called "cluster" sort. They were dull and heavy, and I felt them over my entire head. It was as if I had a lead helmet on that was both heavy and a bit too tight.

I tried as best I could to find out what was wrong with me.

I went to an eye doctor, thinking it might have something to do with my vision. I went to a dentist to check my teeth but also to check for a TMJ disorder, something that was quite the fad in those days. I consulted an eye, ear, nose, and throat specialist. I had my head x-rayed, and although I was surprised to learn that I was missing a frontal sinus, it was unrelated to my headaches. I also sought help from a chiropractor and a naturopath.

None of these doctors or healers could give me a diagnosis, and no one offered a cure. The naturopath suggested that I might be allergic to wheat and peanuts, so I tried dropping those foods from my diet. It didn't help.

After two years living with this chronic pain, I was quite at the end of my rope. The headaches were there each morning as I awoke and lasted all day. I felt as if I couldn't go on, and at one point I just wanted to give up and die. It was that bad. My spiritual beliefs did not permit me the option of suicide, but I did try to bend the rules somewhat. I started walking across the street without looking to see if cars were coming. My thought was that I might get hit by a car and killed, but that it wouldn't technically be an intentional suicide. I know how stupid that sounds, but I was desperate and didn't know what to do. This was in Boulder where traffic was kind of light. No car ever hit me or even came close.

Of course I considered that my headaches might be the ordinary result of stress, but that just didn't make sense. Not only was I trained as a psychologist, I was also specifically trained in stress reduction. I knew how to use exercise, breathing techniques, meditation, body relaxation techniques, visualizations, chi work, diet, and you name it, to counter the effects of stress. I not only knew these techniques, I taught them for many years,

A very bad day

and I used them on myself. In fact, I was the most relaxed person I knew. My headaches were not coming from stress. But just in case there was something I had missed, I joined a gym for the first time in my life and began working out. It didn't help.

My friends started to get concerned about me, particularly my old friends. Those that came to visit could see how badly I was suffering. They also saw that quinoa was all I was interested in, and it was all I talked about. I must have been a bit hard to take back then, and perhaps they thought I'd become pathologically obsessed. I not only ate quinoa, I seemed to breathe it and live for it. It was obvious that quinoa had become my only passion, and I was totally devoted to it. My friends saw all this, and that my health was failing. On bad days I looked as if I were eighty years old.

My friends put two and two together and pleaded with me to quit working with quinoa. They wanted me to leave Quinoa Corporation. They believed that somehow quinoa was killing me, and they tried to convince me to quit. I didn't quit. I couldn't. I felt compelled to do what I was doing, that I had no choice in the matter.

Aside from the headaches, I was never happier than during this period of my life. I was doing what I truly loved. This quinoa business was so much more than a business for me. It was a mission, a calling. It was my life. *If only I weren't suffering with these damned headaches!*

After a while I thought I needed to look in an entirely different sort of direction. *As no doctor, or even healer, could identify the source of my headaches, might they be a manifestation of something non-physical?* I started wondering about a curse, or spell of some kind. *Maybe something to do with quinoa? Or with David?*

I figured that if anyone would know about any sort of meta-physical cause for my suffering, Oscar Ichazo would know. I wrote and asked him if there was something he knew that perhaps I should know. He never wrote back.

I then took this line of thinking a step further. I found an organization in Denver, called in those days the Tibet Foundation. They claimed to be able to read past lives, explain strange happenings, and even cure curses. I arranged for a session with their psychics and explained what I was doing with quinoa, what had happened to Dave Cusack, and what was going on with my undiagnosable headaches.

They told me that my headaches were indeed because of negative forces opposing what I was doing with quinoa. They said my work was critically important for humanity, something truly positive, and that positivity at that great scale is always met with opposing forces, "legions of negativity." They weren't any more specific than that, nor did they use the words "curse" or "spell."

I also learned from them that my connection with quinoa was so strong because it went back to past lives, and that David's past lives were associated with corn, not quinoa. I sort of understood what they were telling me, but it didn't change anything. I still had headaches.

The Cure

Toward the end of 1987 I got a phone call from Silvia, David's ex-wife.

"*Hola querido*. There's a *curandero* in Boulder right now, a Peruvian by the name of Don Eduardo Calderon, and he's going to teach the Naropa students about shamanism, and I'm going to be his translator. I really think you should ask him about your headaches."

My first thought was, *Yeah, sure!* But when Silvia insisted, and told me that Don Eduardo was quite famous in the shaman world, the real deal, I thought I might as well try. It seemed easy enough, as he was staying at a private house not far from where I lived. All I had to do was call and then go there and introduce myself. This is exactly what I did.

The door to the house where he was staying was opened by a young boy, and, when I asked to see Don Eduardo, he told me that his grandfather was sleeping but that I should wait.

It was a little after noon, and apparently my "highly respected shaman" had been drinking wine that morning and was sleeping it off. But after a while, he appeared.

Although Don Eduardo looked exactly like what one might expect—short, dark, rough-looking, and with long black hair tied in a single braid—I was surprised. I imagined that someone as powerful as he was reputed to

Don Eduardo Calderon

be would be more impressive looking. To me, he just seemed rather small. He spoke no English, so I explained why I was there in my faulty but adequate Spanish. I told him about the headaches, my frequent travels to the Andean countries, and my involvement with quinoa.

He brought out a quartz crystal tied at the end of a long leather strap, and held it near various parts of my body, starting at the top of my head. The crystal rotated ever so slightly each time he brought it near me. *"Sus chakras son en revés."* It seems that the crystal turned each time in the wrong direction, indicating that my chakras, my energy centers, were somehow backward. They were in reverse.

He told me he would work with me that evening, and that I must bring *"ron blanco y tabaco negro ... para el diablo."* White rum and black tobacco for the devil! My thought at the time was that they were probably for him, but so what? He wasn't asking me for any money. I found some white rum, and for the tobacco I got a pack of the strongest cigarettes I knew, the French brand called "Gitane."

As I waited for the appointed hour, I began feeling that something important was about to happen. I'd felt that same feeling before when I was about to meet other powerful "spiritual" beings. It was a high-energy, yet uncomfortable feeling. It felt as if the world as I knew it was about to be turned upside down.

I returned that evening carrying the requested objects in a plain brown paper bag. I don't know why, but that seemed like the right thing to do. The bag was taken from me, and I was led to an open area outside, behind the house. Much to my surprise, it was crowded with people.

As it turned out, this was to be a class for the Naropa students, a class on the ways of the shaman, and I would be one of the subjects. Naropa is a liberal arts college in Boulder founded by Allen Ginsburg and the Tibetan Buddhist teacher Chögyam Trungpa in 1974. They teach a wide range of interesting and esoteric subjects. This class, I was told, would run well into the night and possibly early morning.

A typical shamanic table

I walked around a bit, but didn't feel much like socializing with any of the students. At one point I went up to the front where a blanket was placed on the ground. On it were various objects, pieces of metal, stones, amulets, sea-shells, knives, and bottles with unknown liquids in them. This I was told was the shaman's *mesa*, his table, a collection of objects of power. Don Eduardo was later to sit behind this blanket with Silvia at his side as his translator.

The ceremony, or whatever it was, began with preparation of the assembled group, and the setting of a proper atmosphere. I remember drumming, a fire, and a lot of smoke hanging in the air. Don Eduardo himself walked through the group. He put some sort of heavily scented liquid, like a perfume, in his mouth, and then spit it out in a fine misty spray into people's faces and around their heads, two people at a time. This highly unusual act in itself created a strange feeling in me and in the group. *This was not going to be an ordinary evening.*

I was told that the group was supposed to be taking a psychedelic substance, either the hallucinogenic San Pedro cactus, or psilocybin "magic" mushrooms, but that neither was available for that night. What we took instead was a "medicine" he had prepared out of tobacco and various herbs infused for several days in alcohol. A small amount of the liquid was put in a little seashell, and each of us was to pour this very, very carefully into a nostril, and let it drip down the back of our throats. We were cautioned not to sniff or otherwise breathe in the liquid as it would burn terribly. I did as I was told.

Once the group was suitably prepared, the first subject was called, a young woman with some sort of emotional problems. To be honest, I didn't pay much attention, and I don't remember what happened to her, except that it didn't last very long. And then I was called. It was my turn.

I was led into the center of the group in front of the *mesa*. A white circle was drawn on the ground, maybe three or four feet in diameter, using salt. Or perhaps it was sugar; I don't know which. A lot of newspaper was crumpled tightly and placed in the center of the circle and then lit on fire.

Don Eduardo handed me a short sword, which I was to hold in my right hand extended above my head. This sword was one of his most powerful sacred objects and had been used many years ago in a war. It had killed many people. I was to wave it around over my head while I jumped through the fire at my feet. I was instructed to jump in a controlled fashion first along the north-south axis and then the east-west axis. Once again, I did exactly as I was told.

The session began. While I was jumping through the fire in the white circle, Don Eduardo seemed to enter into a trance state and began shouting out loud whatever he was seeing. He wasn't speaking in sentences or rationally constructed thoughts. It was more like flash reports about pictures or images that appeared suddenly in his consciousness. Poor Silvia translated as best she could.

He reported seeing a Peruvian shaman. He saw him conjuring up a curse. He described the shaman's small house on the shores of Lake Titicaca, near the town of Puno, Peru. The curse was about quinoa. He saw David being killed by this shaman's curse. He saw me "sighted down the barrel of a gun!"

The curse was very, very strong, Don Eduardo said, and he called for help to pull it out of me. It was as if he was extracting some sort of evil substance from my body, or a black cloud from my aura. He called to his teachers by name for help. He called out loudly and repeatedly for blessings and protection. He invoked the presence of Jesus and Holy Mary, calling their names over and over. He asked his *"Tia,"* his aunt who taught him about the mushrooms that make you sing, to help him. He also began chanting "Om Mani Padme Hum," the famous Tibetan Buddhist mantra, much to my amusement.

Whatever it was that was happening, it was really intense both for him and for me. I understood it to be some sort of epic battle within the spirit world, shaman vs. shaman, good vs. evil. Silvia later told me that she felt the energies, the poisons he was drawing out of me and into himself, were so dark and evil that she literally feared for Don Eduardo's life.

For my part, I felt exhilarated by the jumping and the fire beneath my feet. I waved the sword as if my life depended upon it. My heart was pounding loudly. I heard Don Eduardo's voice pleading for help over and over. The scene was noisy, intense and chaotic. It felt as if everything was happening all at once.

As I jumped through the fire and fought an unseen enemy with the sword, I felt white light run up my spine, into my head, and then up and out. It wasn't a continuous stream of light, but rather discrete balls of brilliant hot white light, many of them, one after another. Although they were made of light, they had a strong physical presence in my body. There was nothing gentle about it. They traveled up my spine and then disappeared above my head. It was all too much, and I was nearing the border of total collapse. My only thought? *God Help Me.*

I heard Don Eduardo shout, *"Ayúdame! Señor Jesus, Señor Jesus ... Señor Jesus!"*

And then, suddenly ... everything stopped! Just like that, it was all over. Everyone stood there stunned, silent.

Don Eduardo got up, walked quickly back into the house without any explanation, and everyone was told to go home. There would be no further teaching that night.

I staggered to my car, and pulled away. I drove around for several hours in a daze, not knowing what to do or where to go. Finally I went home and tried to get some sleep.

When I awoke in the morning I realized that the headaches

Silvia

were gone. The lead helmet I had carried on my head for over three years had been lifted from me, and I was free. The transformation was as clear as night and day. I didn't yet feel totally "normal," as all that time spent under this apparent curse had weakened me. But the headaches were gone, and as time went on I got better and better. Thank you, dear Silvita!

The Quinoa Curse

After my session with Don Eduardo I felt more than a little confused. I didn't know quite what to believe about what had happened with me, and I was also rethinking why and how David Cusack was killed. I'd just been cured of my "incurable" headaches by a highly respected Peruvian shaman. He said I was under a curse because of quinoa, and he also stated that I had been "sighted down the barrel of a gun," just like David. He attributed David's death to this curse. Don Eduardo saw and reported on all this while in some sort of trance state.

Was this it? Was this the truth behind David's death and my headaches?

I felt confused, but there were also moments when I felt angry at myself for not having seriously considered the possibility of a curse, and for not doing something about it a lot sooner. Had I been smarter perhaps I wouldn't have had to suffer for over three years.

My thinking about this whole experience went on for many months after the ceremony. As difficult as it was to believe Don Eduardo's version of events, I couldn't ignore the fact that he, and only he, had been able to cure my headaches.

In February 1988, I saw the movie "The Serpent and the Rainbow." It was a powerful film that told the true story of Harvard ethnobotanist Wade Davis' experiences with Haitian voodoo. After watching it I realized that things such as curses or voodoo are so far out of the range of ordinary experience that most people, including myself, find it difficult to take them seriously. This, despite the fact that there is plenty of evidence that curses do exist.

O.K., I thought, *Let's take this seriously. I've just gone through a very real experience with a curse.*

Let's just suppose this was a curse. Why? Why would someone put a curse on quinoa? This shaman from Puno didn't put a curse on me personally. He had nothing against me. He didn't even know me. The only motivation that made sense was that he must have been trying to protect his people from what he saw as the greed of foreigners. This, I could understand.

The indigenous peoples of the Andes have been exploited, used and abused by foreigners ever since Francisco Pizarro stepped on Peruvian soil in the early 1500s. The Spanish conquered the whole Inca Empire, stole and then colonized their lands, shipped their treasures, especially gold and silver, back to Europe, and enslaved their people. This abuse went on and on. In later centuries, the mining of tin in Bolivia produced enormous wealth in Europe, but not in Bolivia. Bolivian land produced the tin, Bolivian people slaved in the mines, but the benefit went elsewhere.

The people of the Andes were some of the poorest in the world. I could imagine this shaman thinking, *Enough is enough. No one is going to take our precious quinoa from us. It belongs to us. What comes out of our soil is ours. And certainly no foreigner is going to get their hands on it.*

I understood this line of thinking, but I did not agree with it.

Quinoa is not like gold, silver, tin, or in modern times, lithium. When you take gold out of Andean land, it is gone forever. When you grow a quinoa crop in Bolivia and ship it out, you get to grow another crop the next year, and the next, and the next. Quinoa is a living thing that can be grown over and over again forever, as long as farmers take proper care of their soil and water resources.

When you grow quinoa and ship it out, wealth comes back in, not out. I knew that producing it in the Andes for world consumption would greatly benefit the people of that region, and it has. It has indeed, and it still is!

Furthermore, quinoa is such an important food that it would be unconscionable, perhaps even immoral, to keep it under lock and key, for use only by the citizens of the Andes.

Food should be for everyone, everywhere, rich or poor!

I also wondered why the Tibet Foundation psychics I consulted about my headaches didn't recognize this curse. Probably because it was something that was culturally specific to the Andean peoples. It took someone from the same culture to recognize it, and Don Eduardo was the right one to do so.

Curses are a normal part of Andean culture. You might say that these people are highly superstitious and susceptible to

Talismans and good luck charms for sale in La Paz

shamanic belief systems. All sorts of amulets, talismans and good luck charms are for sale in the back streets of La Paz. No building on the Altiplano can be constructed without a llama fetus buried in a wall. The spirit world is part of their everyday reality.

Llama fetuses for sale

Even Paz, a well-educated, urbane *Chilena*, believed in Andean spiritism. Once, before one of my buying trips, she asked me to get her a Bolivian *Ekeko* statue, a painted ceramic representation of the Tiahuanacan "God of Abundance." She had heard about the power of this figurine in Chile and wanted one for our home in Boulder.

Our *Ekeko* was about eight inches tall and wore blue pants, a red jacket, brown bowtie, black shoes, and a typical multicolored wool *chullo* hat with ear flaps. All around his body were tied miniature representations of various material goods that normal people would wish to own. There was a small ceramic house, a car, a piece of foam representing a bed, rubber sandals, a small straw basket, a bag of flour, Bolivian peso bills, and plastic bags of foodstuffs including pasta, puffed rice, and puffed wheat. I added a little plastic bag of quinoa. All of this was tied to his body with white string.

Ekeko's arms were outstretched, and his hands were in a welcoming position. He had black hair and a thin black mustache, and, quite frankly, he looked a bit seedy, not at all what one would think of as a god of anything.

There was one more important feature of *Ekeko*. His mouth was open and his teeth showed. Paz was told that he loved cigarettes, and that if you gave him one, he would grant you whatever wish you desired.

At the time Paz was tired of her job at IBM and wanted something more

Ekeko, the God of Abundance

interesting and better paying. So she lit a cigarette, put it in *Ekeko's* mouth, and asked him to give her a dream job. Four days later Paz got a great-paying job as private secretary to a rather eccentric multimillionaire businessman. His office was in the Boulder airport, and more than once he took Paz up for rides in his private jet. She was very happy!

Many months later, Paz got the idea that she could ask *Ekeko* for a house for us. We were still living in the confined spaces of an attic apartment. She gave *Ekeko* a lit cigarette and asked him for a house, but this time she got distracted and forgot about him. The cigarette burned all the way down and scorched his mouth and teeth badly. Three days later, for no apparent reason, she got fired from her dream job. And we never got a house.

Can a curse affect someone from a different culture, or someone who doesn't even believe in curses? Apparently, yes. Voodoo is known to work on believers and non-believers alike. Neither David nor I were believers.

Am I now a believer? I don't know. I have no agenda in this matter. I am not trying to convince anyone of anything. All I know is what happened.

This is what happened.

David was the point man in South America on our quinoa project. He was killed mysteriously, and no one could explain how or why it happened. Then I became our point man, and got awful headaches that no one could cure or explain. Then a Peruvian shaman cured me. He said that David and I were under a curse and that the curse was because of quinoa.

In my mind, I can imagine that a rifle was fired into the air from a great distance from where David was standing. Somehow the bullet from that gun was guided to David, to enter his back, pierce his aorta, and kill him. Guided how? By some mysterious shamanic force? Or was it by fate? Destiny? Bad luck? I do not know.

I entered the scene, and I too was "sighted down the barrel of a gun." I was not killed, but was tortured by headaches for over three years, headaches that almost brought me to the point of suicide.

Why did I not also die? Perhaps my many years of spiritual practice made me more resistant to shamanic influence than David. Maybe I had protectors, or perhaps it just wasn't meant to be. I do not know.

Why did I form my hand into a gun and say to Don that "There is only one solution?" Why did my meditation go so very wrong on the day of David's death? I do not know.

There is no scenario, reasonable or not reasonable, that covers all the elements in this strange story. I've stopped trying to figure it all out, and in a way this has liberated me, freed me from thinking that there is always an explanation for everything.

Some things are by their very nature mysterious.

After my experience with Don Eduardo I thought long and hard about the possibility that this curse might not have just touched David and myself. I've heard others, including John McCamant, wonder about this also. One thinks about all the things that have gone wrong and then asks whether they too could be the result of a curse. It seemed to me that there were too many tragedies among the people who worked with quinoa for it to only be a matter of coincidence.

Peter Drake, a friend from the Boulder Arica community, was the one who introduced Don to David Cusack and helped create the plan to grow quinoa in the United States. Peter very much wanted to be a part of the quinoa project, but there was never any obvious role for him to play. Peter was there in the beginning. Much to our surprise, and totally out of character for Peter, he wound up robbing a bank! He got caught and went to jail. While in jail he hid behind a wall and sadly, he killed himself.

Another Arican friend was the first person we hired to work in the warehouse. He was the one who filled our twenty-five pound bags by hand with a scoop and sewed the tops shut. While he was working for us, he got into a traffic incident. The police did a background check on him and found that he'd walked away from an indictment for drug trafficking many years earlier. He'd been a helicopter pilot in Vietnam and later allegedly flew marijuana into Florida. The Boulder police put him back in jail, where he got into some sort of altercation with other inmates. He was pushed off a balcony, fell and broke his back. He's been paralyzed ever since.

The mother of our first receptionist died of cancer while working for us, as did several other people involved with quinoa. John McCamant's wife died of cancer, as did Enrique Espinosa's daughter and later his wife. Rebecca Wood also got cancer and stopped eating quinoa.

Sarah Ward, the Colorado State University quinoa expert, developed a sensitivity to quinoa dust and had to stop working with it. She also suffered tremendously when her technical work breeding quinoa was misinterpreted and she was accused publicly of trying to patent and thereby steal the rights to a certain variety of Bolivian quinoa. The accusations were unjust and the whole incident weighed heavily on her.

Of course there were many, many crop failures. The most notable ones were Julio Torres' disaster in Argentina, and John McCamant's struggles year after year that basically bankrupted him. But there were many more people with high expectations of growing quinoa that also had to give up.

And then there is the story of Don and myself, the story of a once great friendship sadly breaking apart.

Are all or any of these events the result of a curse on quinoa, or are they just part of the ordinary vicissitudes of life? Right after my experience with Don Eduardo I believed that the curse was real and that it might be more wide-reaching than just on David and myself. As I think back on it now, that doesn't seem as likely. I just don't know.

There has never been any suggestion that quinoa itself was cursed or that harm would come to people who ate it. If there was a curse, it was upon the people who worked with quinoa, not on the food itself. To the contrary, quinoa has proven to be a tremendous blessing for all who have eaten it.

CHAPTER SEVEN

My Resignation From Quinoa Corporation

BY THE BEGINNING OF 1988, my headaches were a thing of the past. The incident with the RAM Group had come and gone, and no other buyer for the company was on the horizon. Don and I weren't talking. Great Eastern was unhappy. Quinoa Corporation was continuing to lose money. No one was happy!

I desperately wanted to do something to help. I was still under contract and drawing a salary, with half of it being deferred, but at that point I was not really needed. With all that quinoa I bought from BOINSA, we certainly didn't need any more supply. What we needed were sales, and that was Don's territory. The company needed him, not me. In my thinking it made sense for me to resign in order to lessen the financial burden on the company. So, on the "Ides of March" (March 15th), 1988 I tendered my resignation.

I did not step down from my position at Quinoa Corporation because I was giving up on the company, and I certainly was not giving up on quinoa. I was trying to find a practical solution. I was trying to help. In my mind, the resignation meant that I wouldn't be paid, but I didn't want to cut ties with the company.

Don saw it differently. We weren't on speaking terms, so there was no way for me to explain exactly why I was resigning. One day I went in to the company and discovered that my name had been removed from the mailbox and my office had been rented out. It was terribly awkward.

Don became president of Quinoa Corporation and Dave became vice president in charge of sales. As far as Don was concerned, I was out.

So, what do I do now? My heart still belongs to quinoa. What do I do? I thought I should stick with what I knew best, the supply side of the business; but I didn't want to do anything that would harm Quinoa Corporation. I decided to broker quinoa to a buyer I knew in Germany. At that time there was only one bakery in Germany using quinoa, but my contact and I thought quinoa could go much further than that throughout Europe. It did, but only much later. I operated under the name Gorad & Company and sent shipments to Germany, but unfortunately, I never got paid. There was little recourse for collecting commission money due from a Bolivian seller.

I went to Don and suggested that I become the broker for all future supply to Quinoa Corporation and that Quinoa Corporation be essentially a marketing company. Don said, "No. I have to do what's in the best interests of the company." He used the same reasoning against me that I had used when I decided to go along with the RAM Group and leave Don out. If revenge was what Don wanted, he certainly got it.

Later that summer, without any discussion with me, Don bought Quinoa Corporation from Great Eastern. He gave them back his GEII stock. If rumors I heard were true, Don took upon himself substantial financial burdens in order to keep the company alive, including putting the car he loved so very much up for collateral.

With Quinoa Corporation out of his hair, Sam Simpson steered Great Eastern in an entirely different direction and staked its future on selling Old San Francisco Natural Seltzer, and later Stewarts Root Beer. It turned out to be a good choice for him and his company.

Paz left for New York City to fulfill her lifelong dream of working at the United Nations, and I remained alone in Boulder, waiting and hoping for something to happen.

Quinoa's Unsavory Savior

My waiting paid off. As one of the few experts in the field, I was offered yet another opportunity to work with quinoa, this time through Jack Carasso.

An agronomist and entrepreneur, Jack first introduced himself to me in 1986. He was interested in quinoa and wanted to know about Quinoa Corporation, what we were doing, and what our prospects were. It wasn't clear how he might become involved and at the time we were in talks with Great Eastern, so nothing came of our first meeting.

I saw him again at a Quinoa Growers Conference in the San Luis Valley, a meeting set up by John McCamant to convince more Colorado farmers to experiment with quinoa. I could see that Jack was serious about growing quinoa; he was doing trials in the San Luis Valley, and also in his home state of California. I liked Jack a lot, as we were both deeply fascinated by the technical aspects of quinoa. He and I talked the same language.

Late in the summer of 1988, several months after my resignation from Quinoa Corporation, Jack asked me to join him and a partner in forming a new quinoa company. Jack was planning to grow quinoa and they wanted me to sell whatever he grew. In September I flew out to San Diego to talk with the two of them.

Richard C. Bramson, Jack's business partner, was one of the oddest characters to enter into the story of quinoa. He had heavy, rough features and decked himself out with big gold rings and gold chains. He reminded me of an out of shape version of the actor Charles Bronson and looked like he'd just stepped out of a Hollywood gangster movie. Dick Bramson talked about himself as a savvy, old world California businessman, but quite frankly, he looked more like a crook.

Jack told me that he and Bramson worked as a team and were already partners in a jojoba growing project. He told me I could trust Dick. I liked Jack and trusted him, so I wrote off my suspicions about Dick as mere prejudice and opened myself to the two of them. We talked together over a three-day period, and then I went to Dick's office in Thousand Oaks. The sign on his door said Charles Chase Group, and I wondered who that might be.

I came away from our meetings convinced that I had found an ideal situation for myself, but more importantly, for the future of quinoa. I was impressed with both Dick and Jack. Jack had all the technical expertise one could wish for. Finally I would be working with someone who could actually handle the growing as well as the processing of quinoa. And Dick knew how to structure businesses, raise money, negotiate and write contracts.

During our conversations I spoke about my dissatisfactions with Great Eastern. I complained about Sam Simpson's lawyer-like way of running a business, and about the pressure Great Eastern put on us to produce profits when we were in fact still just a startup company. I talked about how I wanted to see a company managed, and what kinds of people I wanted to work with. Dick responded with a letter, accompanied by a "professional agreement." It skillfully reframed my own business philosophy.

> "It is a concept which primarily stems from my long held personal philosophy and belief that profits, success, and moralities can be synonymous and do not have to be at conflict about each other. It is a concept that is hard for most people to grasp, especially professionals such as lawyers, accountants, stockbrokers, and the like . . . . Also, this concept has in the past and even at present put me somewhere outside the mainstream of the traditional business and investment world, which by the way, doesn't bother me in the slightest."

Dick's letter spoke to me. I trusted both him and Jack.

The agreement Dick drew up spelled out the terms of a working partnership between Gorad & Company and International Inca, Inc., and on October 1, 1988, I signed it. I was impressed at how well the agreement was written and even more delighted by the generosity of the terms. I would get a 20% commission on all quinoa I sold, options to buy up to 25% of International Inca stock at a nominal price, and I would be made an officer in this new quinoa company. I was being offered just about everything I could possibly want. It seemed like a dream come true.

I spoke openly with Dick about how we should proceed. It was obvious to me that instead of starting from scratch, we should try to buy Quinoa Corporation. The company had everything we needed: a well known brand name, a line of products, trademarks, established relationships with distributors, an operating physical plant complete with all necessary cleaning machinery, and the very best name a quinoa company could have.

Quinoa Corporation was still failing and I'd heard that Don was personally liable for its mounting debts. I thought he would be more than relieved to sell.

I also strongly advised Dick to keep David Schnorr, at that time the most essential person in the company. I told him to move the whole operation to California, where there were ports for incoming ocean shipments as well as the major markets for selling our products. There was no longer any need for us to be in Boulder.

Lastly, I told Dick half-seriously that if he bought Quinoa Corporation, he would have everything he needed. And, that he would no longer need me! He laughed, and assured me that I was absolutely essential to the future of the company.

Dick then came to Boulder accompanied by an associate who looked even sleazier than he, and the two of them met with Don. It didn't go well. I knew Don wouldn't like the way these guys looked, and he didn't. Not at all. I had to convince Don that Dick was for real, knew what he was doing, and could very well be the savior that Quinoa Corporation desperately needed, even if he didn't exactly look the part.

And, on the other side, I had to convince Dick to ignore his dislike of Don and concentrate only on the company and what it was worth. Don's dislike of Dick made Dick dislike Don. What a mess! I worked with both of them for most of the month of October. I thought the effort was worth it. Quinoa needed for this to happen. And on my part, I was even seeing myself possibly back as president of Quinoa Corporation.

It was not to be.

On October 28th I received a strange letter from Bramson voiding the "professional agreement" and breaking all ties with me. The letter was full of lies about what I had said and done. At first I was confused and didn't understand what was happening. *Why is he dumping me?*

It all became clear when I learned that International Inca Limited Partnership, another of Dick's legal entities, had made a formal offer, dated November 3, 1988, to buy Quinoa Corporation. Dick did what I half-feared he might do. He followed my advice, bought Quinoa Corporation, and kicked me out.

Many years later I found out that Dick had talked to Dave behind my back. He told him his plan to buy the company, and offered to make Dave the new president. He didn't mention me. Dave then told Don about it when they were together in Baltimore for the Natural Foods Expo. Don recalls Dave being extremely nervous, like "a cat shittin' peach seeds!" Dave thought he was betraying Don and felt horrible about it. Don felt hurt at first, and was in shock. And then, the fire alarm in the hotel went off. It was a scene that neither of them would ever forget! Once this new turn of events sank in, Don thought it might work out to the company's advantage. Dave never knew of my involvement.

Richard Bramson was a crook, a crook that actually looked like a crook. He played me for a fool. And I was a fool.

At one point, recognizing that I was no longer part of the deal, I thought I should at least get a finders fee for making the sale happen. I wrote to Don about this but he once again turned his back on me.

The deal finally closed on March 2, 1989. Once Dick had control of Quinoa Corporation, he did everything I had recommended. He moved the operation to California, and made David Schnorr the new president. Don was allowed to stay on as a board member.

I was still hoping to somehow be actively involved. I wrote to Dick again asking to handle supply for Quinoa Corporation as a broker. I had asked Don previously, when he was in control of the company, and he had said "no." David Schnorr wanted me to handle supply, as that was not something he was comfortable doing. But he told me I had to ask Dick. Dick said "no."

"No, no, no." That was it for me. I was out. Not only was I out, my name was removed from all of the company literature, even from the recipe booklet I had created. They pretended that I had never existed. I thought that odd and rather mean-spirited.

Don was out in terms of day-to-day management of the company, but he was still very active as a board member and was collecting money from the sale. He worked with Dave at trade shows, did product development, package design, recipe development, graphic design, record keeping, and served as an advisor. But Quinoa Corporation, for all practical purposes, was now in the hands of David Schnorr, and there it would remain for more than twenty years.

In May of 1989 I went to a lawyer to see if I could sue Dick Bramson. It was the only time I've ever gone to a lawyer for anything. The lawyer looked through all the letters and contracts I had saved and saw that I had clearly been wronged. Just from my appearance and demeanor he thought a jury would easily come out in my favor. My lawyer got quite excited, as he was sure we

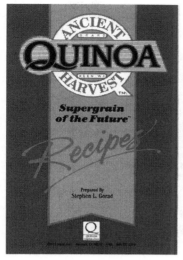

My recipe booklet

would win, and win big. But several weeks later, after he'd researched Bramson, his tricky maneuvers, and the variously named business entities he used, he declined to take the case. Although he was sure we'd win, he was equally sure that we'd never be able to collect a dime from Bramson.

As time went on, Dick and Jack had a falling out and sued each other in the fall of 1991. I was called by Jack's attorneys to testify about the unsavory nature of business with Dick. I did so happily. In 1996 Don got paid the final installment of the money owed to him from the sale of Quinoa Corporation. Somewhere along the line Dick Bramson disappeared from sight. Dave Schnorr couldn't find him. He was later confirmed as dead. Jack Carasso also later died.

Quinoa Corporation Lives On

Dave Schnorr, the new president of Quinoa Corporation, reassembled the company in California completely on his own,

David Schnorr at work

a testament to the depth of his appreciation for and dedication to quinoa and his considerable management skills. Dave was a salesman, but now he had to do everything. Machinery was disassembled, moved, and put together in a warehouse in California. An office was created with only one person to help him. Sales and marketing efforts continued uninterrupted. And Dave learned, with no help from me, how to get supply out of Bolivia.

Dick Bramson left Schnorr alone to manage Quinoa Corporation and concentrated on what he knew best, how to put money into his own pockets. He sold shares of the company to about thirty naive individual investors and kept their money for himself.

Dick wasn't interested in the success or failure of Quinoa Corporation, but David was. He cut spending to a bare minimum, at first making just enough to cover salaries for himself and his assistant. Sales grew slowly but steadily. Gross revenues finally crossed the one million dollar mark in 1994. By 2001 they were $6 million. And from that point on sales continued to grow year after year. Quinoa Corporation finally became a success story!

With Dave at the helm, the company provided a steady stream of quinoa for more and more people to learn about, to try, to eat, and to enjoy.

The growth of the company was not without challenges, of course. In 1996, the largest natural food distributors merged, giving them the clout to buy quinoa directly from South America. This move eliminated the market for Quinoa Corporation's twenty-five-pound bulk bag. Dave made up for the loss in business by creating totally new quinoa products, including the now very popular red and black quinoa.

David went to Bolivia and continued the work I had started, buying from ANAPQUI, the largest quinoa cooperative with the most advanced processing operation. When ANAPQUI decided they'd rather sell at higher prices to Europeans in 2006, David responded by working with Javier Fernandez to create Andean Valley, and a new state-of-the-art quinoa processing and exporting facility. Andean Valley has grown and prospered since then and continued as the most important supplier of Bolivian organic quinoa *real* to Quinoa Corporation.

David Schnorr shepherded the growth of Quinoa Corporation from 1989 until 2013, when he sold it to Encore Consumer Capital, a company that had the management expertise and financial resources to try and take Quinoa Corporation to a whole new level. In the hands of Encore's people, the Corporation began creating and marketing many forward-looking new quinoa products, perfectly suited for

Dave in 2013

the next generation of health-conscious consumers. Under Encore's management Quinoa Corporation definitely moved on to new territory.

During all the years Dave had the company, he and I spoke frequently on the phone about all things quinoa, and I was always trying to drum up new business for him. He graciously kept me supplied with quinoa for personal use at cost. Although I had no formal or financial interest in Quinoa Corporation during Dave's tenure, I always felt extremely protective of it. Once it was sold to Encore, however, it felt a little like the company had grown up and moved on.

I had finally lost my "baby."

CHAPTER EIGHT

Quinoa Lives On

DON AND I STARTED OUR work with quinoa in the late 70s, and we founded Quinoa Corporation in 1983. I was out of the company by 1988, and Don a year later. During that brief, yet tumultuous, period of time, we succeeded in taking quinoa out of total obscurity and placing her firmly on the starting line of an ever-expanding path toward worldwide use and recognition.

Quinoa, of course, had been grown and eaten for many thousands of years by the indigenous peoples of the Andean Mountain regions of South America. We totally recognize that quinoa belongs first and foremost to them, and it always will.

What Don and I did was to create Quinoa Corporation, and as a result quinoa became available to people in the United States, then in Europe, and now the rest of the world. We were the first to recognize quinoa's greatness and enormous potential for good, and to do something about it. Through our efforts, and those of David Schnorr, quinoa's popularity grew, but it grew slowly. Because of our activities, other companies started importing and selling it, and its popularity grew even greater. More and more people got to eat quinoa, like it, and tell others about it. Quinoa spread primarily through word of mouth. Now, over thirty years later, quinoa is known throughout the world, and its popularity is still growing.

For me, quinoa crossed an important milestone when it was served (as quinoa risotto) to world leaders by President George W. Bush on November 14, 2008, at a White House State Dinner during the G20 Economic Summit. Imagine my delight when I learned that quinoa, once considered dirty, poor peoples' food suitable only as feed for chickens, was served, eaten, and enjoyed by the likes of Nicolas Sarkozy, Angela Merkel, Silvio Berlusconi, Hu Jintao, Gordon Brown, Dmitry Medvedev and many others, all leaders from around the world. I still can't help smiling when I think of this.

Meeting Bolivian President Evo Morales at the UN

Quinoa has more recently enjoyed a truly phenomenal jump in popularity. The United Nations FAO declared 2013 the "International Year of Quinoa." This great honor did not cause the rather sudden, recent explosion of worldwide interest in quinoa, but it was an important part of it.

Many other factors were at play. Over the years, systems for producing and distributing quinoa got better and better. Farming practices in South America slowly improved. Processing technology advanced greatly. Sophistication in business improved with the years, as did modernization of export facilities and logistics. The

Modern quinoa field

movement against eating gluten in the United States gave quinoa a big marketing boost, as quinoa is gluten-free. All of these factors,

Modern processing technology

and many others, contributed to quinoa's recent rise in popularity.

Quinoa passed yet another milestone when Dana Milbank wrote in the March 15, 2013 edition of *The Washington Post*, "But this time they also tasted the clumpy quinoa of self-doubt and the curdled soymilk of recrimination." Although an unflattering image for quinoa, Milbank's sentence indicated to me that quinoa was now a recognized enough part of popular culture to be used as a metaphor.

New knowledge and new perspectives about the unique importance of quinoa are continuing to come to light. As quinoa becomes better and better known, it is being researched by younger and perhaps even brighter minds. For example, in the November 11, 2013 *New Yorker* article, "Climate by Numbers," Michael Specter quotes the young CEO of the Climate Corporation, David Friedberg.

Modern export facility

"'The ratio of protein to energy used to produce quinoa is the highest of any food source,' he told me, and then launched into a detailed and impassioned description of how the world would feed itself in the coming decades. 'You just have to do some simple math,' he said. It is a phrase he uses a lot, although his math is almost never simple. 'The net energy utilization of the protein production of beef is fifty to one; for fish it's ten to one, and for chicken it's four to one. Soybeans are two to one —they're pretty efficient, but quinoa is less than one and a half to one, and quinoa grows in all these drought-hardy conditions. There is all this land that's undeveloped—in Saskatchewan, in Colorado, in large swaths of Peru—and the yield that you can start to get on quinoa if you start to invest in production would be substantial.'"

"If quinoa replaced meat as the principal source of protein in developing countries, 'it would lower greenhouse emissions sharply,' he said. 'And radically cut back on our use of water. But that is not where we are currently headed.'"

These new perspectives on quinoa's greatness are very exciting, and relevant to issues of the day. Among Friedberg's many important points, I particularly like the one about undeveloped land.

Quinoa is a non-competitive food crop. It will grow where no other food crop can survive. In fact, some of the best lands for growing quinoa in the United States are places where there are currently no farms or farmers, or even roads—high mountain grazing lands and high altitude deserts.

Friedberg, incidentally, went on to buy into Northern Quinoa Corporation, Canada's most important quinoa growing and marketing company. And he also founded, with partners, a fast growing restaurant chain called Eatsa. Eatsa serves customized "quinoa bowls" using an innovative fully automated delivery system.

As a result of an unprecedented jump in popularity beginning in 2013, quinoa also underwent a period of rather difficult growing pains. As demand increased precipitously, and supply remained constricted, prices rose dramatically. When I was buying Bolivian white quinoa back in the 80s we paid around $1,000/metric ton, sometimes as little as $800/metric ton, and I thought those prices were unreasonably high. In 2014 that same quinoa was selling for over $7,000/metric ton. These prices had little to do with production costs. They were due to supply and demand, and more than a little bit of greed.

The good news is that because quinoa suddenly became such a valuable crop, everyone everywhere wanted to grow it. Quinoa farms have been popping up in Canada, the western United States, Australia, France, Spain, Tasmania, India, and even such unlikely places as UAE, Thailand, Egypt, and China. At this point it is unclear how many of these projects will actually succeed. As years go by, the list of countries trying to grow quinoa gets longer and longer.

Plant scientists at the Wageningen University in the Netherlands bred new strains of quinoa that are better adapted to

European growing conditions. They also bred out the bitter coating, which means that it does not need saponin removal processing. This quinoa has been cultivated for several years in the Loire Valley in France and has recently become a popular variety for farmers in Great Britain.

Back in South America quinoa started being planted in non-traditional areas. It has been tried in Argentina, Uruguay, and in low elevation areas of Peru. By far the greatest recent increases in production have been in Peru. Farmers who used to grow vegetable crops in coastal regions switched to quinoa and had to use chemicals—mainly pesticides and fungicides—to get a decent yield. Some of that quinoa had chemical residues on it and was rejected at the United States border. Rumors spread about contaminated quinoa. Some rumors were true, and some were just attempts by traders to gain an advantage by bad-mouthing their competitors. Things got rather ugly for a while.

As a consequence, prices for quinoa from some sources plummeted back down to between $1,000 and $2,000/metric ton. Sometimes these savings were passed on to consumers, but more often they were not. Good people with good quinoa got caught in price squeezes, and many went out of business. There is still a lot of instability in the quinoa markets. But these problems are just signs of growing pains, and they will be worked out over time.

Another of quinoa's growing pains involved the media backlash begun by Joanna Blythman's 2013 article in the *Guardian*. She wrote, "In fact, the quinoa trade is yet another troubling example of a damaging north-south exchange, with well-intentioned health- and ethics-led consumers here unwittingly driving poverty there." Once this unfortunate misinformation was published, it spread like wild fire through social media.

Let me state that Blythman's facts and premise are just plain wrong. Other reputable writers have countered her arguments point by point; but every now and then her misinformation gets repeated as if it is real.

It should be noted that the jumps in prices, and thus in profits, benefitted for the most part the farmers themselves. The indigenous farmers and their cooperatives, particularly in Bolivia, saw demand for their quinoa going up, so they asked more for their crops, much more, and they got it. And once again, I must say that I can't fault them for this. They live in an uncertain world where it makes sense to get as much as you can in the present moment.

The growth in quinoa's popularity, especially now that it is grown on non-traditional lands, has created yet another issue. Back when the only source for quinoa was Quinoa Corporation, there was only one variety of quinoa you could buy, the large white Bolivian organic *"real."* Later, red and black quinoa were introduced, again by Quinoa Corporation. These were the only known varieties in the U.S. for many years.

The reality is that there have always been many different varieties, sizes, shapes, and colors of quinoa, literally thousands of them. When we first started, people in South America said the best was *quinua real*, or royal quinoa. We accepted this as fact, and decided to sell only the best. By doing so, we established the large white quinoa grain as the standard for the industry. Objectively speaking, there is no "best"

Bolivian quinua real

quinoa. They are all a little different, and some are very different, like the southern Chilean sea-level varieties. But they all
are good. Once we started with the large white grain, we had to
continue with it as our regular product.

But these days, you never know what you are getting when
you buy quinoa. The package may say "product of Peru," but
you won't know if it is from the traditional highlands or some
other part of Peru, and you certainly won't know the variety.
Some packages say "product of the Andes Mountains," which
could even mean Ecuador or Colombia.

Why is this important?

Because different kinds of quinoa cook differently. Some
quinoa cooks up light and fluffy, others are kind of crunchy,
and others are by their very nature mushy or even sticky. The
Northern Quinoa Corporation in Canada has been growing and
selling a very tasty variety that originated in southern Chile. It
is distinctly different from Bolivian, as it is smaller, darker, and
very sticky.

A while back there were people writing and arguing about
how to cook the "perfect" quinoa. Dan Souza at America's Test
Kitchen studied quinoa very carefully and published in the Jan-
uary/February 2014 issue of Cook's Illustrated the recommenda-
tion that quinoa should be cooked with only one part water to
one part quinoa, half the water we originally recommended. I've
tried it, and it works! The problem is that this may work well
with some quinoa, but it won't work with all varieties. As more
farmers produce quinoa on different lands, there are going to be
many more variations in the cooking properties of quinoa.

Not only will these different types of quinoa cook differently, they will also taste different. Some are bland by their nature,

but others are earthy, and some others are very earthy. Yet they are all just sold as quinoa. People will be confused until they learn that not all quinoa is the same. All of these types of quinoa, no matter the variety or where it is grown, are good as long as they maintain quinoa's excellent nutritional profile.

A Staple Food for the Future

These problems are all just symptoms of growing pains in the early years of a life that will go on far into the future. Quinoa is a staple food that will be more and more important as time goes on. It could be providing real solutions to many of the world's most vexing problems, including climate change, food insecurity, and depletion of water resources. And yet, some people mistakenly think of quinoa as just a fad.

Quinoa will eventually be mass produced and become a commodity like rice or wheat. It will be in our bread, pasta, baked goods and breakfast cereals. There might even be quinoa oil, but perhaps with a different, clever name, on the oil shelves at your local supermarket. Quinoa germ, as a nutritional supplement, may someday appear in the market, as will quinoa protein concentrates. And perhaps protein-rich quinoa leaves will be grown and sold much like spinach. Components of quinoa will certainly be used in non-food products; the oil and saponin in cosmetics and shampoos. Perhaps the starch will find a place in industrial processes.

Plant breeders, and yes, genetic scientists, like it or not, will create improved varieties of quinoa. The quinoa genome has already been decoded, and scientists are now talking about creating varieties without the bitter saponin and also those that can tolerate high temperatures during the growing season. These modifications, combined with quinoa's innate hardiness, salt tolerance, and low water use, will allow quinoa to be grown almost anywhere in the world. Indeed, as Don and I predicted, quinoa will be the "supergrain of the future."

That all aspects of work on quinoa continue is important, because quinoa is just too good as a food and as a crop to be ignored.

While this is going on, the original quinoa varieties will still be grown in Bolivia, and in the highlands of Peru, Ecuador, Chile, Argentina and Colombia. It will still be grown organically and sold to discriminating consumers in the United States and the rest of the world. These original varieties will also be planted on small farms in remote parts of the world, where nutritional resources are scarce, and farming difficult. It will be produced and used much like it is in Bolivia or Peru. It will not only feed humans, but the leaves and stalks may also serve as food for animals.

While no food can or should be touted as perfect, it has been said that quinoa comes as close as any other food, if not closer, be it from vegetable or animal sources. Nutritional analysis of quinoa attests to its extraordinary quality.

Of course, an indigenous person living in the Andes wouldn't be interested in what scientific assessments of quinoa have to say. He knows that quinoa provides him with the energy and strength to endure the oxygen-poor air and bitter cold of the mountains and high plains where his people have survived for centuries. The Andean peoples know that quinoa is a plant of unusual vitality. It is a true survivor, too, in the midst of a very difficult world.

Where does a plant put its strength and vitality? In its seed, of course! The eating of this tiny seed is the Andean peoples' key to a vigorous, healthful life. And it is that for us, as well.

The unusual strength of the life force in the quinoa seed is clearly evidenced by certain of its unique properties. Quinoa germinates far more quickly and easily than any other seed. Quinoa will germinate after two to four hours in a glass of water, whereas it takes a wheat kernel twelve hours. It is as if quinoa is just waiting to explode into growth. And once it starts growing, it is difficult to stop. Sprout makers know that placing mature sprouts of any kind in a refrigerator will end their growth. This is not true of quinoa sprouts. They will continue to grow even in the deep cold of refrigeration.

This life force is what makes the original highland quinoa, and in particular *quinua real* from the exactingly harsh environment of the southern Altiplano, so special. From a vital energy perspective, this is without doubt the very best quinoa.

I expect that quinoa eventually coming out of other lands with equally severe growing conditions, like Tibet, will be just as excellent. These truly miraculous plants, those that grow where nothing else will grow, produce quinoa with the most powerful energy. This level of excellence could even be achieved in the United States, in the high mountains where at present there are no farms or farmers.

Quinoa's roots reach deep into the past, but its vision projects headlong into the future. In today's world of ecologically delicate and highly specialized food crops, quinoa stands tall as a wild, and as yet untamed, resource. It is an unusually strong plant that produces an exceptionally nutritious food.

Quinoa's importance lies not in its exotic past, but in its worldwide potential as a staple food for the future.

Quinoa in Tibet

Although the high Tibetan Plateau provides its inhabitants with an exquisite world of natural beauty, it offers severely limited and meager resources for the support of human life. Despite an area approximately equal to that of Western Europe, Tibet has a mere 215,000 hectares of arable land. The limiting factors are average elevation of 14,800 feet, low rainfall, short growing season, and extremes of temperature. In short, from the point of view of the farmer, Tibet is a high, frigid desert. Doesn't this sound familiar? Since Tibet shares many of the agroclimatic conditions of the Andes, one might think that Tibet would be ideally suited for growing quinoa. I had that thought, and so did Gongbu Jashi.

As a young agronomist at the College of Agriculture and Animal Husbandry of Tibet, Gongbu Jashi fortuitously attended an agronomic seminar in Mexico in 1987. There he met Octavio Moreno, someone I had helped test quinoa in Mexico. Octavio introduced Gongbu to quinoa, gave him some seed, and told him about me. Back home in Tibet, Gongbu wrote me, asking if I thought quinoa would grow in his native country.

I was so happy when I read his letter. I'd dreamed of seeing quinoa growing in Tibet, and now I had the opportunity to do something about it. Even before Quinoa Corporation began slipping away from me, the Tibet project became very dear to my heart.

Of all the places on this planet that quinoa might belong, Tibet was at the very top of my list.

I knew that the high Tibetan Plateau, also known as the "Roof of the World," would be both an exciting and challenging place to try quinoa. The one major food crop cultivated successfully by the Tibetans is barley, from which they make *tsampa* (toasted barley flour and yak butter tea), their staple food. Where barley grows, quinoa also tends to do well, and because of its unusual hardiness, quinoa could very well be an even better crop for Tibet than barley. Land that cannot support a barley crop, land at the highest altitudes, with very little rainfall, or where the soil is excessively alkaline, could be perfectly suited for quinoa production. This, of course, would need to be proven through year after year of test plantings.

I sent Gongbu all the information we'd researched and compiled, along with Duane Johnson's growing instructions based on Colorado State University's experiments. I'd been collecting seed from South America wherever and whenever I could, so by then I had a rather diverse quinoa seed bank, which I always distributed freely to anyone who asked. I sent Gongbu a little of just about everything I had as there was no way for us to know which variety would succeed. Gongbu would eventually try all the varieties I sent him. His first trial planting was in 1988.

I wrote up a "Quinoa in Tibet" project proposal to formalize what we were trying to do. In it I explained how similar the Tibetan Plateau was to the Bolivian Altiplano. It also struck me that the people from these two parts of the world looked very much alike. I put photos of Andean people and Tibetans in the pamphlet, and when I challenged people to tell which was which, it was hard for them to see the difference.

I even sent a copy to the Dalai Lama, and asked him for a letter of support. In a "Statement" dated September 19, 1991 His Holiness wrote:

> "I am happy to know that in keeping with the Buddhist precepts not to harm or kill sentient beings, Dr. Stephen L. Gorad

and his group are starting a project called QUINOA IN TIBET in the hope that more Tibetans may be able to adopt a vegetarian diet."

After five years of success with test plantings Gongbu felt confident that we were on the right track. Quinoa could work as a new crop for Tibet. He wrote saying it was time for me to come visit and see for myself how much quinoa loved being in Tibet. *Yes!* I jumped at the chance to go.

But it wasn't so easy.

In 1993 there were only two ways into Tibet—flights from Chengdu in China, or from Kathmandu in Nepal. Traveling through China by myself to Chengdu seemed daunting, so I chose Kathmandu. Gongbu wrote me that there were flights from Kathmandu to Lhasa every Wednesday. He said he was sure the only flights were on Wednesdays. I had to rely on Gongbu for this information, because in those days travel agents in the U.S. weren't able to book travel into Tibet.

After a long, difficult, tiring flight from New York, with a stop in Dubai, I arrived in Kathmandu on a Monday, expecting to fly to Lhasa on Wednesday. I rested that night and went to the Southwest China Airline office early the next morning. What greeted me was a sign in the window saying, "Closed – Will Reopen Thursday."

What?!!

With the office closed until Thursday, how do I fly out on Wednesday? I'm doomed! I'll miss the only flight to Tibet. There I was, halfway around the world in Nepal, in a place I didn't want to be, and already I was in deep trouble.

My preconception about Nepal was that it would be somewhat like Tibet, as it was also a Himalayan country. My imagination expected to find cold, a vast beautiful emptiness, and very few people. But when I got to Kathmandu, it was hot, dirty, and crowded, much like India. I'd gotten very, very sick in India years before, and I didn't want to repeat that. I was not at all happy with conditions in Nepal, feared for my health, and was anxious to move on.

Kathmandu

Alone, tired, confused, and feeling extremely disoriented, I walked over to a small cafe, ordered a cup of tea, and sat there praying that I would get into Tibet. I rarely pray for myself, but in that moment I prayed to be allowed to continue my journey.

I spent the rest of Tuesday and Wednesday as a reluctant tourist in Kathmandu. When I got to the airline office again on Thursday, it was open, and I was told there was a flight leaving that very night. I happily signed up for it, but I was concerned about what I'd do when I arrived in Lhasa.

There was no way to contact Gongbu and he had expected me the previous day, on Wednesday. Without him there in the airport as my official sponsor, I wasn't going to be admitted to the country; one couldn't just fly in without an approved host. I had no phone number for Gongbu, only a mailing address. I didn't even know his correct name, as his letters came to me variously signed Gongbu, Gong Bu, Gonbu, or Gongbo as his first name, and Jashi, Trashi, or Zhaxi as his last. Obviously, there was a Tibetan to English translation issue.

When my flight landed in Lhasa, there was Gongbu in the airport, with a big happy smile on his face, and a small delegation to greet me. I breathed a long sigh of relief, and passed through immigration easily. After the customary handshakes with the waiting group and a hug with Gongbu, I asked him why he had told me the only flights were on Wednesdays.

He nodded, "Yes. Today. Wednesday."

Oh, no!

Gongbu didn't know which English names went with which days of the week.

This instance of totally screwed-up communication set the stage for the rest of my stay in Tibet. From that day on, I never knew where we were going, nor what was happening. Nobody spoke English, so I had to rely on Gongbu's broken English. But it really didn't matter, as he never told me what we were doing or why. I just went where they took me and did what they asked me to do. I was like a blind man being led through a magical journey in Wonderland.

Of course, it all turned out just fine.

After spending a few days in Lhasa, so I could adjust myself to the high altitude, we drove to Nyingchi in eastern Tibet, where the agricultural college was located. I later found out that the Nyingchi region of the country was off limits to foreigners. No westerners had ever been allowed there, but I don't think my hosts knew that.

I was checked into a bare bones hotel. In my room was a small tin of instant coffee. The hotel staff thoughtfully calculated that, being an American, I couldn't survive without my coffee.

Each night they brought me four huge thermoses of hot water. The hot water was so I could make myself coffee, but it was also for washing. There was no sink, shower, or bath. There was no running water. There was a bathtub, with a worm-like creature crawling around in it, and a western-style toilet, but without a seat. Both were totally useless without running water. I was to learn that washing wasn't as necessary as I previously believed.

It was October, because I wanted to be in Tibet at harvest time, and the high-altitude, thin air was cold, very cold. The hotel had no heat, but instead, my bed had a stack of blankets about two feet high. It was awkward trying to sleep under the weight of so many blankets, but I managed, and I kept warm enough. The cold also made washing a lot less attractive.

Every morning a Chinese woman came to get me. With hand gestures and Chinese words that I couldn't understand, she escorted me downstairs to the kitchen where I was served a

Tibet from 20,000 ft.

truly excellent Chinese-style breakfast. There were many different delicious dishes, and I always ate a lot. It was quite a funny scene, watching myself gorging on food while little pigs ran around at my feet on the dirt floor.

Each day we traveled to the quinoa fields in jeeps, and at one point we drove through a pass at over 20,000 feet elevation. The view was spectacular, a wide river valley below and magnificent snowcapped mountains towering in the distance, just like in pictures. We stopped to rest at a place with snow on the ground and hundreds of Buddhist prayer flags fluttering in the wind. My hosts kept looking at me to make sure I was all right. They were concerned that this fifty-one-year-old American might pass out in the oxygen-poor air, or God forbid die. But, quite the contrary, I felt really good up there.

As we drove from quinoa field to quinoa field, what I found was the most beautiful quinoa I'd ever seen. The sight of row after row of robust quinoa plants towering over me, with seed heads of gigantic proportions, yaks grazing nearby, and the snowcapped Himalayas surrounding us, was something astonishing and unforgettable.

Quinoa not only grows well in Tibet, in many instances it grows better there than it does in South America. On the Bolivian Altiplano the plant rarely stands more than a scrawny two or three feet tall, but some of this quinoa was over six feet high, huge, lush, and overflowing with seed. It was as if quinoa had come home, as if it belonged in Tibet.

Quinoa growing in Tibet

Gongbu grew test plots in Nyingchi, near the college where he taught, and in the surrounding area. There were plots in Shigatse, in western Tibet as well. We traveled to all the sites where quinoa was growing, and several times we went way beyond where government regulations allowed. I stood out like a sore thumb, and of course caught the attention and concern of

Tibetan quinoa field

local police. Once, they confiscated my passport, but they didn't seem to know what to do with it, so they let me go.

We talked to many farmers. Not all of the quinoa was growing equally well, and because I never knew what was planted where, I couldn't figure out which seed varieties were producing best. The usual bitter saponin coating on the grain somehow wasn't appearing on the Tibetan grown quinoa, and that was great news, as removing it wouldn't be an issue. Saponin hadn't been on the Mexican quinoa either. None of us knew why this was so. I was asked to cook some of the Tibetan quinoa for a formal tasting event and everyone agreed that it was more than excellent.

I gave a lecture at the college, translated by an English teacher at the school. I told the audience that quinoa should be developed as a Tibetan crop to be used to feed the local population. It was obvious that Tibetans could benefit from more nutrition in their diet. But like most people in the world, the Tibetans were not particularly adventuresome about food, and I found little interest among the people in eating quinoa. Yes, they were interested in growing it, but not so excited about eating it. I suggested using

Lecture at the college

it to make noodles, as Tibetans were already eating noodles and were importing Chinese rice and wheat to make them. But what they really wanted to do was sell me quinoa and get dollars.

Gongbu understood my way of thinking and agreed that Tibetan quinoa should be used to feed Tibetans. Maybe later, when they could produce an export quality product, a clean grain free of stones and dirt, they could think about shipping it out to

Tibetan seed head full of grain

the United States. Besides quality of product, there was also the issue of transportation. Back then there was no railroad in or out of Tibet, and quinoa would have to be shipped by truck into China, then to a port, and then to the States. Export wasn't commercially practical at that time. But I told them that if they wanted to sell their quinoa, they should promote it in China as baby food. The Chinese could have only one child per couple, so it seemed obvious to me that they'd love to have healthy quinoa baby food.

My visit to Tibet was under the auspices of a Tibetan science commission of some sort. The head of the group, a Tibetan, accompanied us on many of our trips to the quinoa fields. He wore a suit jacket with the manufacturer's label on the outside bottom of the sleeve. I didn't know why

Gongbu and Leonardo

the label was on the sleeve or why he didn't remove it. The label said Leonardo in bold letters, so I called him Leonardo.

Leonardo wasn't the real boss. The person who was actually responsible for me was a Chinese gentleman, Mr. Yongsi Zou, who appeared to be the head of the Nyingchi regional government. Mr. Zou took me to visit many villages in the area, although I never knew why. Each time we entered a village, the entire population came out to greet us, and then we would have a meal together with a select group of people. At each and every meal, and sometimes between meals, we had to drink alcohol, and we had to smoke cigarettes. Almost everyone I met offered me a cigarette, and I quickly realized that to refuse would be an insult. That was it. Arrive in town, meet everyone, take a group photo, shake hands, have lunch, *ganbei* (cheers), smoke, and move on.

Village gathering

One lunch in Lhasa, however, was very different, unusually elaborate, even including vegetarian dishes made specially for me. Gongbu knew I was vegetarian, and he had tried to make sure there was always something I could eat. But this lunch was clearly special. I was to meet with someone special, but no one told me who he was, or why we were meeting him. All I could see was that the food was great, the room kind of fancy by Tibetan standards, and the important gentleman was Chinese, young and exceptionally good looking. As we greeted each other, we exchanged business cards as a formality. I didn't have a chance to really look at his.

The young man told me that he had been receiving reports from Gongbu about quinoa for quite some time, but that he never considered them important. Now that he was meeting me, he realized that quinoa was a serious matter. He said he would pay careful attention to whatever Gongbu did in the future. Furthermore, he promised that he would do whatever he could to advance our project. I liked this guy, whoever he was. After the lunch was over I looked carefully at his business card and saw that I'd just had lunch with Wang Jian, the Vice Secretary General

Ganbei (cheers)

of The People's Government of the Tibet Autonomous Region. He was the governor of all Tibet, or something like that.

As I was deemed an honored guest, Mr. Zou asked me if there was anything I wanted to do or see during my stay in Tibet. I told him I wanted to visit some Buddhist monasteries. When we were in Shigatse he took me to one of the biggest and most important monasteries, Tashilhunpo, founded in 1447 by the first Dalai Lama and the seat of the Panchen Lamas. It was

The great Tashilhunpo Buddha

still almost completely intact. All the Tibetan monasteries we visited were very strange places. They were dark, lit only by yak butter lamps, smoky, dirty, and yet with rooms containing beautiful colorful thangkas of Buddhist deities and gorgeous statues of Buddha covered in gold leaf. The one at Tashilhunpo was an amazing twenty-six meters high.

As we walked around the rooms at Tashilhunpo, I saw out of the corner of my eye several of our group, Chinese Communist Party officials and Tibetans, with their palms together praying and bowing to some of the Buddha images. When we finished the tour and went outside, I noticed that everyone had big wide smiles on their faces. The whole group was obviously very happy!

The Abbot of Tashilhunpo Monastery

I learned that none of them had ever been in a temple before that moment. They were all raised as atheists. To me, their transparently joyful response to the Tashilhunpo Buddhist monastery demonstrated that you can't kill the spiritual heart of people. You can suppress it, but you can't kill it. That made me so happy.

I left Tibet full of big ideas and a lot of hope, hope that the project would progress, that quinoa would soon be growing year after year in Tibet and feeding its people. But the reality was that nothing much happened. The local marketing never went anywhere. Yes, there was some activity at first. Government money, as promised by Wang Jian, was allocated to the quinoa project, and a manager was hired. Gongbu later informed me that the manager took the quinoa money, invested it in some sort of real estate deal, and lost it all.

Gongbu continued with test plantings for many years, but then some years he had to be elsewhere, and there was no one else to carry on. But he always managed to get enough planted to keep the seed stock alive. This situation continued until recently when a successful Chinese businessman from Xi'an expressed an interest in quinoa. He met with Gongbu many times. The more he learned about quinoa the more serious he became, and eventually he even built a quinoa processing plant on his property.

Gongbu Jashi

In October 2011 I traveled to Xi'an to meet him and see his processing plant. Despite the fact that I was impressed with him and everything I saw, progress once again moved slowly following that visit.

Test plantings continued in Tibet and were also tried in China's Qinghai Province, which is contiguous with the Tibetan Plateau, but mistakes were made, and weather conditions created unexpected problems. There were problems with equipment, and as always there were problems with people, and with management. Producing quinoa is not always a simple matter.

Quinoa growing projects keep rising and falling according to circumstances. There have been lots of failures of quinoa projects throughout the world, and Tibet has had more than its share of difficulty. Gongbu, to his credit, has persevered over the long haul, and the outlook at present looks extremely good. Thirty-four metric tons were harvested in 2015, with an average yield of over three tons/hectare, far outstripping typical yields in Bolivia and Peru.

The quinoa plant loves Tibet. That is certain. I saw it with my own eyes. One day, perhaps very soon, Tibet will be producing some of the world's very best quinoa. It is as inevitable as quinoa herself.

CHAPTER NINE

Looking Back

I'VE OFTEN ASKED MYSELF THE question, *Why me?* I seem like an unlikely candidate for doing what I did with quinoa. I wasn't an agronomist, a farmer, or a businessman. I wasn't a chef or a food writer. I was a meditator and was once a psychologist, but what does that have to do with quinoa?

Perhaps quinoa found me because my lifestyle left so many possibilities open all the time. Nothing ever tied me down for long—no career, no relationship, no job, no location. So when quinoa came along, it was quite easy for me to drop everything else I was doing and devote myself to it one hundred percent.

And perhaps my training in living in the moment made it possible for me to move quickly and navigate all the changes quinoa demanded of me. I don't know.

If I look back, I could see that perhaps there were "signs" of what was to come.

I've always been fascinated by food, and by cooking. That is for sure! But I never thought of making my love of food into a career. I cooked for friends and sometimes groups of friends.

That was it. And when I lived in Chile and wrote for *Clan Familiar,* a national woman's magazine, many of my articles were about food.

Looking back

All my life I've also been fascinated by plants. My father was a farmer when he was a young man. I was born on the farm, but then moved to New York City when I was three. Perhaps my father passed his love of growing plants on to me. Tending a vegetable garden has been a rare and great joy for me. I still get excited whenever I see endless fields of food plants growing on farms, and getting to walk through one of those fields is always even more thrilling. I've always surrounded myself with plants wherever I've lived, even now in my tiny Manhattan apartment.

When I was in High School, of all the many things I could have done for the Science Fair, I chose to do an experiment on hydroponic growing of lima beans. I found the whole subject of seeds and how they grow totally captivating.

At one point in my life most of my doodles looked curiously like sprouting quinoa, and this was way before I'd ever heard of quinoa.

So, there were "signs," but nothing truly compelling. Do "signs" reveal destiny? I don't have an answer to that one.

Please understand that when I'm asking "Why me?" I am not implying that it was all or only me. None of this quinoa story would have happened without all the pieces of the puzzle falling together, quite mysteriously, at the proper time. Nothing would have happened without Paz, and without all the other people showing up exactly when they were needed. But mostly, none of this would have happened without Don McKinley. Without him, I would not have done what I did. And without me, he would not have done what he did.

Before we ever started working with quinoa, Don and I talked about doing business together, and in fact we tried the Lambsbread Woolens business, and failed. It just seemed natural that we should do something together. Around that time, we played with the idea that whatever we did, it would be under the name "Castor & Pollux." Castor and Pollux are the Gemini twins in the zodiac, one mortal, one divine, and we kidded each other as to who was which. My birthday falls on June 16th and Don's on June 14th, both in the sign of Gemini, so it was obvious to us that we were the Gemini twins.

When I think back on it, Don's reasons for working with quinoa may have been somewhat different from mine. We both recognized the special importance of quinoa, and wanted people to know about and use quinoa, but Don's focus was more on achieving success in the world of business than mine was. Perhaps he was also more focussed on succeeding in life than I was. It certainly seems that way in retrospect.

I think Don was born appreciating and wanting to have things of quality in his

Don looking great

life. Even when I first met him, when he was jobless and poor, he wore only the finest clothes, and of course always looked great. He was the first person I'd ever met who knew about and bought designer brands. In contrast, I always wore t-shirts and blue jeans, and still do.

It was the same with cars. During our Quinoa Corporation years Don drove a gorgeous, British-racing-green Jaguar, whereas I had a badly painted, old brown VW Rabbit. After the Rabbit broke down, Don found me a used, gray Mercedes-Benz sedan. I must say I loved driving the long empty roads to the San Luis Valley at a hundred miles per hour, with cruise control on, and my feet up. Ah, thank you, Don!

It is clear to me that what we did with quinoa would not have happened without the blending of energies flowing out of the two of us. Nothing would have happened without the down to earth, practical knowledge of business and fierce determination to succeed that Don contributed. It seems that simple good intentions are not enough in this material world; desire is a necessary ingredient for success. Nothing would have happened without my deep love for quinoa and my so-called "spiritual" energy that perhaps invited grace into the enterprise. Both were needed. Both of us were needed.

And what about David Cusack? David's short story is perhaps the strangest of all. His contribution to quinoa was also absolutely necessary, at the beginning. And then, it wasn't. I don't know what else to say.

Lovers of Quinoa

I was recently in Bolivia and met with Dr. Juan Risi, for many years the head of IICA (Inter-American Institute for Cooperation on Agriculture) in Bolivia. We were sitting in a cafe, having a bite to eat and talking about the many people who are now involved with quinoa. I was mentioning names of people I'd met at the International Quinoa Research Symposium, the first of its kind in the United States, organized by Dr. Kevin Murphy and held at Washington State University in August 2013.

Juan made a distinction between those people who are self-less servants of quinoa and people who are using quinoa for their own ends. Some people are so taken by quinoa that they wind up devoting their lives to doing whatever must be done in the service of quinoa. Other people are riding the wave of interest in quinoa and are using it to further their own careers, to make a name for themselves, or simply to make money.

I liked Juan's distinction. It was clearly accurate, but it wasn't always easy to apply. Sometimes it is impossible to determine why anyone does what they do. *And in the end*, I thought, *does it really matter? Quinoa benefited, no matter what.*

There are, however, several individuals that should be acknowledged for their undisputed selfless service to quinoa.

Humberto Gandarillas Santa Cruz is considered by many to be the father of quinoa in Bolivia. I never had the pleasure of meeting him, but I heard his name mentioned probably more than any other when I worked in Bolivia.

Ingo Junge Rodewald, a professor at the *Universidad de Concepción*, Chile, did important early research on quinoa and wrote the seminal monograph, "Lupine and Quinoa Research and Development in Chile" (1973), that answered my first questions about quinoa.

Jaime Alba was a central figure in the formation of the first Bolivian quinoa cooperative called in those days *Operación*

Tierra, but now known as CECAOT. He helped me a lot during my early visits to Bolivia.

Mario Tapia is considered by many to be the father of quinoa in Peru. Mario came to help us in Colorado, and has been a champion of quinoa throughout many decades.

In 1986, during one of my many visits to Ecuador, my brother-in-law Capi arranged for me to give a talk to landowners and farmers about the importance of quinoa. It was held in a large tent out in the fields. I remember distinctly that I grew impatient with my translator, and much to my surprise, started speaking in Spanish. It seems that when the subject is quinoa, I can speak fluently in English or Spanish. As usual I spoke with great enthusiasm about my very favorite subject. There was only one person in the audience that day who listened to my words and took them seriously. That was Rodrigo Arroyo.

Rodrigo fell in love with quinoa. He planted it, learned everything he could about growing it and processing it, and in

Mario Tapia, myself,
Rodrigo Arroyo, Gongbu Jashi

1989 formed his own quinoa company, INAGROFA. He has been in the quinoa business ever since, with many ups and downs. Rodrigo devoted his life to quinoa. Based on real, hands-on experience, Rodrigo is the one person who can be said to be today's expert on all things quinoa.

Of course there is John F. McCamant, who headed

John McCamant

Sierra Blanca Associates after David Cusack died and partnered with Ernie and Paul New at White Mountain Farm in Colorado, where quinoa has been planted every year since 1986. Once "caught" by quinoa, John, although often times reluctantly, devoted the rest of his life to getting quinoa growing in the United States.

Juan Risi Carbone is another of the quinoa greats. Juan received the first Ph.D. for research on quinoa at Cambridge University in 1986 and has continued to promote quinoa development throughout his remarkable professional career ever since.

Sergio Núñez de Arco is a more recent member of the quinoa lovers group, having started his company in 2004. He is a founder and current CEO of Andean Naturals, a company devoted to helping Bolivian farmers produce and sell only the finest organic *quinua real*. His company is a member of the "Fair Trade Federation," and Sergio can be found traveling all over, tirelessly promoting his beloved quinoa.

Quinoa Has a Life of Its Own

All of these men worked selflessly and tirelessly for the benefit of quinoa, and I too devoted a good part of my life to quinoa. It started for me on that auspicious day back in my friend's kitchen in Santiago, Chile. What a strange and powerful moment! Cooking and then eating quinoa for the first time was a life-changing experience for me. It felt as if I'd fallen in love.

But perhaps it was quinoa that was doing it all. Did I "fall in love" or did quinoa somehow seduce me into becoming her servant for life?

What ensnared Sergio, Rodrigo, Juan, or the others? Was it fascination, obsession, or what? I don't think they themselves knew. The truth is that once caught by quinoa, they just couldn't forget her, and neither could I.

I'm sure John McCamant wouldn't have called his capture by quinoa a love experience. He even spoke of it as a "burden" that had been laid upon him. In a chapter called "Quinoa's Roundabout Journey to World Use" in *Chilies to Chocolate: Food The Americas Gave the World,* John wrote:

"In the past five years I have learned to appreciate an early quinoa advocate's remark that 'Quinoa has a life of its own.' Quinoa seems to use people rather than the other way around. As some have become disheartened, quinoa has attracted new people to take over. Spirits of the Andes may have placed all kinds of obstacles in the path of those trying to preserve and disseminate the 'mother grain,' but it seems destined none-the-less to take its rightful place among the crops of the world."

I was that "early quinoa advocate." To me, it always seemed as if quinoa was the active agent. She's been fulfilling her destiny through people like us who for one reason or another are drawn to serve her.

I said that quinoa has a life of its own and that she finds people to do what needs to be done. John McCamant took that to mean that quinoa "uses" people. I don't know how this actually operates, nor how to speak properly about it, but I do strongly believe that there is more going on than what meets the eye.

I was delighted to see Michael Pollan write in a far more intelligent way than I ever could about this very subject. In *The Botany of Desire: A Plant's-Eye View of the World*, Pollan asked if plants use humans as much as we use them.

> "These plants hit on a remarkably clever strategy: getting us to move and think for them. Now came edible grasses (such as wheat and corn) that incited humans to cut down vast forests to make more room for them; flowers whose beauty would transfix whole cultures; plants so compelling and useful and tasty they would inspire human beings to seed, transport, extol, and even write books about them. .... That's why it makes just as much sense to think of agriculture as something the grasses did to people as a way to conquer the trees."

Pollan also wrote about how there is much more to plants than what we may realize. Who is to say whether plants or people are more evolved?

> "Plants are so unlike people that it's very difficult for us to appreciate fully their complexity and sophistication. Yet plants have been evolving much, much longer than we have, have been inventing new strategies for survival and perfecting their designs for so long that to say that one of us is the more 'advanced' really depends on how you define that term . . . ."

Pollan showed in his book how the apple, tulip, marijuana, and potato in particular use the human desires for sweetness, beauty, intoxication, and control respectively to create more of themselves and further their own survival.

This made me think, *What is the key to quinoa's success?* What does she offer to make us do her will? Quinoa doesn't have a particularly exciting taste and it definitely isn't sweet, beautiful or intoxicating. What is it about quinoa that makes people want to eat it, and certain people to fall in love with her, or become obsessed by her?

Could it be that our bodies' need for real nourishment is what makes quinoa so attractive, and makes some of us servants of quinoa's need to propagate herself throughout the world?

Perhaps quinoa is in fact the one food designed by nature to perfectly nourish the human body.

Perhaps quinoa truly is miraculous.

In Closing

Many people have assumed that because I was a founder of Quinoa Corporation, the company responsible for introducing quinoa to the world, I must have become wealthy. They are surprised when I tell them that I didn't. By all the usual measures in the arenas of business, fame and fortune, I did not succeed. But quinoa has! And that has always been the only thing important to me.

My love for quinoa did not end after I left Quinoa Corporation, and neither did my efforts on her behalf. I stayed active and involved in many different ways. I continued at times to use business as the vehicle for getting things done. I never used quinoa to do business.

Was this overly idealistic of me? Naive? Perhaps, but I think not.

At M.I.T. I attended a lecture by Buckminster Fuller, the unconventional visionary and inventor of the geodesic dome. He told us he always did what he thought was right, right for himself, but more importantly right for humanity, and never ever concerned himself with making money. He said that if you follow that path, you will always have exactly what you need, but nothing extra. You won't have money in the bank, but whatever you need will come at just the moment you need it.

"Bucky" Fuller taught me to focus on doing what was right and not worry about money.

Joseph Campbell, teacher, lecturer and author of *The Power of Myth*, expressed the same life philosophy, in a different way. In *The Hero's Journey* (p. 217) he wrote:

"I have a firm belief in this now, not only in terms of my own experience, but in knowing the experiences of other people. When you follow your bliss, and by bliss I mean the deep sense of being in it, and doing what the push is out of your own existence - it may not be fun, but it's your bliss, and there's bliss behind pain too."

"You follow that and doors will open where there were no doors before, where you would not have thought there'd be doors, and where there wouldn't be a door for anybody else. There's something about the integrity of a life. And the world moves in and helps. It really does."

"And I think the best thing I can say is to follow your bliss. If your bliss is just your fun and your excitement, you're on the wrong track. I mean, you need instruction. Know where your bliss is. And that involves coming down to a deep place in yourself."

I learned from these and other teachers that if you focus on doing what is right, discover and follow your own particular bliss, your life will have an adventurous yet harmonious quality to it. Nothing that you truly need will be lacking.

I also learned from my teachers and from my experiences working with quinoa that life basically takes care of life. Be still, be open, and let life go where it wants to go. Stop worrying, stop judging, stop planning obsessively, and stop trying

Flying off into the future

to predict each and every outcome. Let your life live you. It will flow from, and in a sense belong to, something beyond and infinitely greater than the you that you think you are. Life will flower of its own accord, and be full of mystery and yes, miracles. There will be challenges, but it will feel perfect, and you will find yourself smiling quietly inside!

I'd like to thank you for taking this journey into the early years of quinoa with me—through the ups and downs of business and friendship, in and out of encounters with odd people, a mysterious murder, a curse, a very strange tale, and adventures in foreign lands. I hope you enjoyed reading about it as much as I enjoyed living it.

I really did enjoy living it!

Thank you.

APPENDIX

I. Quinoa Technical Data

Quinoa (pronounced keenwa) has been called a "super-grain" and one of the few almost perfect foods. The grain is the seed of the plant *Chenopodium quinoa* Willd. It is a member of the Amaranthaceae family and the "goosefoot" subfamily that also includes sugar beets, beetroot, chard, and spinach. It is one of about 250 species of the genus *Chenopodium* which can be found all over the world. The common weed, lambsquarter, is also a chenopod (*Chenopodium album*) and shares the characteristic goosefoot shaped leaf. Lambsquarter can be found just about everywhere, even in cracks in the sidewalks of New York City. Other edible chenopods include canihua (kaniwa) (*Chenopodium pallidicaule*), which grows in the Andes at even higher altitudes than quinoa, and huauzontle (*Chenopodium nuttaliae*), which was grown by the Aztecs, and is still used today in Mexico.

Although quinoa is grown, stored, and used as a grain, some do not consider it a true cereal grain like rice or wheat, as the plant is a broadleaf and not a grass. It this respect it is sometimes referred to as a pseudocereal. Quinoa also differs from the true cereals in that one plant can produce a very large number of new seeds. Whereas one wheat seed produces about ten new seeds, one quinoa seed produces a plant bearing over a thousand new seeds.

Quinoa is an annual herb and varies in height from twenty centimeters to over two meters (sometimes reaching three meters), depending upon the variety, and where and how it is grown. The stalk of the plant is thick, strong and woody, and the root system can extend as deep as the stalk is tall. The quinoa plant can be highly branched or not, depending on variety and sowing density. The growth cycle can vary from 150 to 220 days.

Quinoa grain forms in seed heads at the ends of stalk branches, somewhat like millet or sorghum. The seeds are small (between one and four millimeters in diameter), round, and somewhat flat, kind of like a tiny hockey puck. They are mostly off-white in color, although some species are white, pale yellow, pink, orange, red, brown, purple, gray, or even black. Their weight ranges from between 250 to 500 seeds per gram. The seeds are covered with a netlike honeycombed pericarp containing a saponin rich (2% to 6%) resin.

II. Nutritional Charts

A. Nutritional Analysis of Quinoa

	Percent (%)* Min. - Max.
Water	9.4 - 13.4
Protein	11.0 - 21.3
Fat	5.3 - 8.4
Carbohydrate	53.5 - 74.3
Ash	3.0 - 3.6
Crude Fiber	2.1 - 4.9

*According to various researchers
Source: Junge, Ingo. *Lupine and Quinoa Research and Development in Chile*. Anales
Escuela de Ingenieria Pub. No. 1 Universidad de Concepcion, Chile, July 1973

B. Nutritional Analysis Comparisons

	Percent (%)					
	Water	Protein	Fat	Carbohydrate	Fiber	Ash
Barley	11.1	8.2	1.0	78.8	0.5	0.9
Buckwheat	11.0	11.7	2.4	72.9	9.9	2.0
Corn	72.7	3.5	1.0	22.1	0.7	0.7
Millet	11.8	9.9	2.9	72.9	3.2	2.5
Oats	12.5	13.0	5.4	66.1	10.6	3.0
Quinoa	11.4	16.2	6.9	63.9	3.5	3.3
Rice	12.0	7.5	1.9	77.4	0.9	1.2
Rye	11.0	9.4	1.0	77.9	0.4	0.7
Wheat	13.0	14.0	2.2	69.1	2.3	1.7

Source: After "Fact Sheet" by Stephen L. Gorad quoting U.S. Department of Agriculture
figures compared with average values for quinoa (Boulder, Colorado, 1976),
Unpublished

C. Essential Amino Acid Pattern (g/16g N) of Quinoa Compared to Wheat, Soy, and FAO Reference Pattern for Evaluating Proteins

	Quinoa	Wheat	Soy	FAO (1973)
Isoleucine	4.0	3.8	4.7	4.0
Leucine	6.8	6.6	7.0	7.0
Lysine	5.1	2.5	6.3	5.5
Phenylalanine	4.6	4.5	4.6	
Tyrosine	3.8	3.0	3.6	
Sum of Phenylalanine and Tyrosine	8.4	7.5	8.2	6.0
Cystine	2.4	2.2	1.4	
Methionine	2.2	1.7	1.4	
Sum of Cystine and Methionine	4.6	3.9	2.8	3.5
Threonine	3.7	2.9	3.9	4.0
Tryptophan	1.2	1.3	1.2	1.0
Valine	4.8	4.7	4.9	5.0

Source: Johnson and Aguilera, *Processing Varieties of Oilseeds (Lupine and Quinoa)*. Table 6 (report to Natural Fibers and Foods Commission of Texas, 1979-80).

III. References

Cook, O.F. *Staircase farms of the ancients; astounding farming skill of ancient Peruvians.* The National Geographic Magazine Vol. 29 No. 5; May 1916: pg. 510

Cusack, David F. *Quinua: Grain of the Incas.* The Ecologist, Vol. 14, No. 1, 1984: 21-31

Eiselen, Elizabeth. *Quinoa, a Potentially Important Food Crop of the Andes.* Journal of Geography, 55, October 1956: 330-333

Junge, Ingo. *Lupine and Quinoa Research and Development in Chile.* Anales Escuela de Ingenieria Pub. No. 1 Universidad de Concepcion, Chile, July 1973

Kellogg, John Harvey. The New Dietetics, What to Eat and How; a guide to scientific feeding in health and disease. Battle Creek, Mich., The Modern Medicine Publishing Co. 1921: pg. 255

McCamant, John. *Quinoa's Roundabout Journey to World Use* in Chilies to Chocolate: Food The Americas Gave the World. Eds. Nelson Foster & Linda S. Cordell, The University of Arizona Press, 1992

Pollan, Michael. The Botany of Desire: A Plant's-Eye View of the World. Random House 2001

Torres, Julio. QuinoaCorp. El Emporio Libros, Córdoba 2006

Underexploited Tropical Plants with Promising Economic Value. National Academy of Sciences. Washington, D.C. 1975

Wood, Rebecca T. Quinoa The Supergrain: Ancient Food for Today. Japan Publications April 1989

Quinoa Cook Books:

Green, Patricia and Hemming, Carolyn. Quinoa 365: The Everyday Superfood. Murdock Books Australia 2011

Polisi, Wendy. The Quintessential Quinoa Cookbook: Eat Great, Lose Weight, Feel Healthy. Skyhorse Publishing 2012

STEPHEN L. GORAD

IV. Resources
Bolivian Sourced Quinoa

Quinoa Corporation
1722 14th Street, Suite 212
Boulder, CO 80302
Phone: (310) 217-8125
http://www.ancientharvest.com

Andean Naturals
529 Ontario Ave.
Sheboygan, WI 53081
Phone: (920) 395-5035
          (888) 547-9777
info@AndeanNaturals.com
http://www.andeannaturals.com

Andean Valley
Av. Panamericana Nro. 1959
Rio Seco - El Alto - Bolivia
Phone: 591-2-2863058 / 2862853
info@andeanvalley.com
http://www.andeanvalley.com

I Heart Keenwah
PO Box 180032,
Chicago, IL 60618
Phone: (844) 533-6924
          (917) 699-7863
ravi@iheartkeenwah.com
http://www.iheartkeenwah.com

Ecuadorian Quinoa

Rodrigo Arroyo
INAGROFA
PO Box 17116650
Panamericana E35 km 24.5
Parroquia Pifo, sector Oyambarillo
Quito Ecuador
Phone: 593-999-735009
www.inagrofa.com
rarroyo@inagrofa.com.ec

Colombian Quinoa

Prime Foods
Calle 137 # 12 - 25 Oficina 101
Bogota, Colombia
Phone: 57-1-626-0129
http://www.primefoods.co/index.html

Canadian Quinoa

Northern Quinoa Corporation
3002 Millar Ave.
Saskatoon, SK Canada
S7K 5X9
Phone: (306) 933-9525
        (866) 368-9304
http://www.quinoa.com

United States Quinoa

White Mountain Farm
Mosca, Colorado 81146
Phone: (719) 378-2436
http://www.whitemountainfarm.com/index.html

Other Quinoa Agricultural Resources

For information on growing quinoa in the **Pacific Northwest** contact:

> Dr. Kevin Murphy
> Washington State University
> 273 Johnson Hall
> PO Box 646420
> Pullman WA 99164-6420 USA
> Phone: (509) 335-9692
> kmurphy2@wsu.edu

For **garden quantities of quinoa seed** contact:

> Frank Morton
> Wild Garden Seed
> PO Box 1509
> Philomath, OR 97370
> Phone: (541) 929-4068
> https://www.wildgardenseed.com

For information about quinoa grown in **Europe** and **Britain** contact:

> http://www.abbottagra.com

For information about quinoa in **Australia** contact:

Jono Semmler

Keenwah

Building 17, Suite 1717

The Entertainment Quarter

Moore Park, NSW 2021

Phone: (02) 9332 4437 or 04338 18412

info@keenwah.com.au

http://www.keenwah.com.au

For information about quinoa activities in **Bolivia** and **Peru** contact:

Dr. Juan Jose Risi

Calle Trípoli 270 - 402

Lima 18, Peru

Phone: +51 - 997149351

juan_risi@yahoo.com

For information about quinoa activities in **Pakistan** contact:

Dr. Hassan Munir

Department of Agronomy

University of Agriculture

Faisalabad, Pakistan 38040

hmbajwa@gmail.com

V. Recipes

None of my "recipes" should be considered actual recipes meant to be followed to the letter. I don't know how to follow a recipe myself, and I certainly don't know how to write one. I am always experimenting. When I shop I buy whatever looks good to me in that moment, without necessarily thinking that it is needed for a particular dish. When I go in the kitchen to cook, sometimes I have an idea of what I want to make, but sometimes I don't. Often I get my ideas from looking at what is there, and what might go well together. Sometimes I don't know what I am making until it is done. When I put together a dish, I never measure anything. I just add whatever seems right to me. Sometimes dishes turn out bad, sometimes good, and sometimes quite excellent. No dish has ever turned out exactly like the last time I made it. No matter what, I serve and eat whatever I have made. It is all food, whether it tastes or looks like it is "supposed" to.

So please, in the recipes that follow, take them with "a grain of salt," as they are really only suggestions. Feel free to change ingredients and quantities. Be experimental. Find out what works for you and for the loved ones you are cooking for.

Quinoa balls

1. Basic Recipe

1 cup quinoa

2 cups water (or as little as 1 cup water)

The amount of water you use depends on the particular variety of quinoa you have, and the end result you are looking for. In general, for quinoa with firm separate grains, use less water.

Basic cooked quinoa

Some quinoa needs rinsing, but many brands do not. You will learn which is which with experience. When I have a quinoa that does need rinsing I prefer the swishing method. I put the quinoa and water together in a 1 1/2 quart sauce pan and measure with my finger how high the water should be. Then I add a lot more water and swish it around to wash the quinoa. Then I pour the water off, and repeat until the water runs clear. Lastly I again use my finger to get just the right amount of water in with the quinoa. Alternatively, you can rinse the quinoa in a fine strainer.

Bring the quinoa to a boil. Reduce heat to a low simmer, cover, and cook the quinoa until all the water is absorbed. This should take about 15 minutes. Midway through the cooking stir the quinoa with a spoon. The quinoa is fully cooked when it has turned from white to translucent, and the germ has separated somewhat. If you are using less than the two to one water to quinoa ratio, let the quinoa rest covered in the pot for an additional 5 minutes then fluff up with a spoon. Makes about 3 cups.

2. Quinoa Bread

    3 cups quinoa flour
    6 cups whole wheat flour
    2 packages dry active yeast
    1/4 lb butter, melted
    3 cups water
    1/4 cup brown sugar
    1/2 Tbs salt
    1/2 Tbs anise, ground

If you can't find quinoa flour, you can grind your own in a high speed blender.

Mix all ingredients together, adjusting the amount of whole wheat flour so you get a not too sticky bread dough. Knead, form into a ball and let rise. Punch down, and divide into three loaves. Place in greased 9 x 5 inch loaf pans, and let rise. Bake at 350 degrees F (175 degrees C) for 25 to 30 minutes.

This is an adaptation of a traditional Bolivian recipe.

3. Little Quinoa Breads

    2 cups quinoa, cooked (mashed)
    1 cup oil
    1/2 cup brown sugar
    1/2 Tbs baking powder

Mix all ingredients to make a dough. Roll the dough out flat. Cut into 12 pieces using the rim of a glass. Bake at 350 degrees F (175 degrees C) until puffed up and browned.

This is an adaptation of a traditional Bolivian recipe.

4. Quinoa Porridge

1 cup quinoa
2 cups water
1 cup milk
1/2 tsp cinnamon
pinch salt
brown sugar or honey to taste

Mix all ingredients. Bring the quinoa to a boil. Reduce heat
to a low simmer, cover, and cook the quinoa until soft. This
should take 15 to 20 minutes. Before serving add brown sugar
or honey to taste.

This is an adaptation of a traditional Bolivian recipe.

Quinoa porridge

5. Quinoa Soup

1/2 cup quinoa
1/2 cup onions, diced
1/2 cup carrots, diced
4 cloves garlic, chopped
oil for sautéing
1 lb potatoes, diced
1/2 cup peanut butter
6 cups water
1/2 tsp ground cumin
1 tsp paprika
1 cup peas
1 cup milk
1/2 cup cheese (queso fresco), diced
1/2 cup scallions, chopped
1/4 cup parsley, chopped
salt and pepper, to taste

Sauté onions, carrots and garlic in a little oil, then add quinoa and lightly sauté. Add potatoes, peanut butter, cumin, paprika and water and simmer until quinoa is cooked and potatoes are soft. Add peas and cook until just tender. Add cheese and milk. Before serving add scallions and parsley, and salt and pepper to taste.

This is an adaptation of a traditional Ecuadorian recipe.

6. Chicha de Quinua

2 1/2 cups quinoa flour

5 liters water

1 Tbs yeast (beer making variety)

4 cloves

4 pieces cinnamon

3 cups brown sugar

To make quinoa flour:
> Wash 2 1/2 cups quinoa.
> Let germinate.
> Dry in the sun.
> Toast in frying pan without oil.
> Grind into flour.

Mix flour, cloves and cinnamon in water. Boil for 1/2 hour. Strain and let cool. Place liquid in large jar and add yeast. Let ferment for 4 days. If fermentation seems slow add some pieces of pineapple or sugar cane. After fermentation add brown sugar. Serve cold.

This is a traditional Peruvian recipe. The original, truly authentic method of preparing the quinoa involves chewing it and then spitting it out into the fermentation jar. I can't recommend that. In fact, I can't recommend this recipe at all. It seems overly ambitious, and results are not guaranteed. Proceed at your own risk.

7. Quinoa Leaf Salad

> 1 bunch quinoa leaves
> 2 medium red or white onions, slivered
> 2 large tomatoes, cut in pieces
> 1 cup grated cheese
> 2 eggs, boiled, sliced
> 1/4 cup parsley, chopped
> Mayonnaise
> Salt to taste

If quinoa leaves are not available, lambsquarter leaves may be substituted. Combine and arrange ingredients according to one's own artistic sensibilities.

This is an adaptation of a traditional Ecuadorian recipe.

8. Fried Quinoa Balls

> 2 cups quinoa, cooked
> 2 eggs, beaten
> 1/4 cup onion, chopped
> 1/4 cup parsley, chopped
> 1 tsp salt

Combine all ingredients, and form into 1 inch balls. Deep fry until golden brown. Drain on paper towel.

For this dish you will want moist quinoa that sticks together well, so use more water when cooking the quinoa. Or, if you can find it, use quinoa from southern Chilean seed (e.g. from Norquin) as it is naturally more sticky.

Vegans can leave out the eggs. The quinoa will still stick together if cooked just right.

9. Locro de Quinua

1 cup quinoa
4 cups vegetable stock or water
1 lb butternut squash, diced
4 medium potatoes, diced
1 cup corn kernels
1/2 cup green peas
1/2 cup carrots, diced
1 cup onion, diced
2 cloves garlic
oil for sautéing
1/2 cup evaporated milk
1 cup cheese (queso fresco), diced
1 tsp oregano
1/4 cup parsley, chopped
salt and black pepper to taste

Sauté onions and garlic in a little oil, then add quinoa and all the other vegetables except the peas, and lightly sauté. Add stock or water and simmer until quinoa is cooked and vegetables are soft. Add peas and cook until tender. Add cheese and milk. Before serving add oregano and parsley, and salt and pepper to taste.

Locro de quinua

This dish is adapted from a traditional Peruvian recipe.

10. Quinoa Vegetable Soup

4 cups water
1/4 cup quinoa
1/2 cup carrots, diced
1/4 cup onions, chopped
1/4 cup sweet red pepper, diced
1/4 cup celery, diced
1/4 cup mushrooms, diced
2 cloves garlic, chopped
1/2 cup tomatoes, chopped
1/4 cup potato, diced
2 tsp salt
cilantro or parsley, chopped as garnish
salt and black pepper to taste

Combine all ingredients except the cilantro and parsley in a large pot and bring to a boil. Reduce heat and simmer about 30 minutes, or until all ingredients are tender. Garnish with cilantro or parsley. Add more salt and crushed black pepper to taste. Serves 4 to 6.

With this soup you can add small amounts of just about any vegetable you might have. Or use fewer ingredients for a simpler soup. Adding 2 Tbs. of nutritional yeast will give the soup a nice chicken-like taste.

Quinoa can be added to just about any soup, but be aware that the longer you cook it, the more the quinoa expands. Cook it for a long time and the quinoa will fill the pot. Sometimes I just add a little cooked quinoa to a soup after it is cooked.

11. Quinoa Croquettes

2 cups quinoa, cooked
2 cups potatoes, mashed with skins
2 eggs beaten
1/4 cup onion, chopped
1/4 cup parsley, chopped
1 tsp salt
1/2 tsp cumin
1/2 tsp black pepper, crushed

Combine all ingredients and form into 1 x 2 inch croquettes. Deep fry until golden brown. Drain on paper towel.

For this dish you will want moist quinoa that sticks together well, so use more water when cooking the quinoa. Or, if you can find it, use quinoa from southern Chilean seed (e.g. from Norquin) as it is naturally more sticky.

Vegans can leave out the eggs. The quinoa will still stick together if cooked just right.

Quinoa croquettes

STEPHEN L. GORAD

12. Quinoa Tabbouli Salad

5 cups quinoa, cooked (cooled)
1 cup parsley, chopped
1/2 cup scallions, chopped
1/2 cup carrots, chopped
3/4 cup pine nuts
2 cloves garlic, minced
1/2 cup black olives, sliced
1/2 cup lemon juice, fresh squeezed
1/4 cup extra virgin olive oil

Combine all ingredients.

There are many excellent variations to this recipe. Add or subtract ingredients as you wish.

For this dish the firmer quinoa works best, so use quinoa cooked with less water.

Firm cooked quinoa is an excellent addition to almost any kind of salad. Try it in chicken or tuna (or vegan chicken or tuna) salads.

Quinoa tabbouli salad

A Few Personal Favorites

Quinoa Chocolate Cake

> 2 cups quinoa, cooked
>
> 1/3 cup milk (or almond, soy, rice milk)
>
> 4 whole eggs
>
> 1 tsp vanilla extract
>
> 3/4 cup melted butter or coconut oil, or any combination of the two
>
> 1 cup brown, coconut or date sugar
>
> 1 cup unsweetened cocoa powder
>
> 1 1/2 tsp baking powder
>
> 1/2 tsp baking soda
>
> 1/2 tsp salt

Preheat oven to 350 degrees F. Lightly grease two 8-inch round or square cake pans. Combine the quinoa, milk, eggs and vanilla in a blender. Mix together the sugar, cocoa, baking powder, baking soda and salt in a bowl. Add the wet ingredients and mix well. Divide the batter between the 2 pans and bake for 40 to 45 minutes or until a knife inserted comes out clean. Cool before serving. Frost if desired.

For this dish you will want moist quinoa, so use more water when cooking the quinoa.

This recipe is adapted from the cookbook *Quinoa 365: The Everyday Superfood* by Patricia Green and Carolyn Hemming. Their idea of using cooked quinoa was simply brilliant.

Back in the beginning days of Quinoa Corporation I made a quinoa chocolate cake with quinoa flour that I made in a blender and brought it to the office for everyone to try. In a few minutes all that was left were a few crumbs on the plate and big smiles on everyone's faces. I had the feeling that we had just crossed over into some sort of new territory. Desserts are supposed to be eaten in small quantities because although they taste so good, they aren't usually that healthy for you. But a cake made out of quinoa is probably the healthiest thing you could eat, so eating more is a good thing. Quinoa chocolate cake just turned our world upside down.

Quinoa Corn Bread

> 2 cups corn meal
> 1 cup quinoa meal
> 1 tsp salt
> 1/2 tsp baking soda
> 1 1/2 tsp baking powder
> 1 Tbs honey or brown sugar
> 1 large egg, beaten
> 3 Tbs melted butter
> 2 1/2 cups buttermilk

Grind raw quinoa in a blender to make quinoa meal.

Mix wet ingredients together. Mix dry ingredients together.

Combine the two. Bake in greased 9"x9" pan or muffin tin at 425 degrees F for about 25 minutes, or until golden brown.

Quinoa corn bread

Quinoa Corn Chowder

1/4 cup quinoa
1/2 cup potato, cubed
2 Tbs carrot, diced
1/4 cup onion, chopped
1 1/2 cups corn kernels
2 cups water
2 cups milk
1/4 cup parsley, chopped
salt and black pepper to taste
butter

Simmer quinoa, potato, carrot and onion in water until soft (about 20 minutes). Add corn and simmer another 5 minutes. Add milk and bring just back to boil. Season to taste. Add parsley and a bit of butter just before serving.

I particularly like that this dish combines quinoa, corn and potatoes, all foods native to South America.

Quinoa corn chowder

Quinoa Pancakes

    2 cups buttermilk (or 2 cups milk plus 1 Tbs apple cider
        vinegar)
    1 cup whole wheat flour
    1 cup quinoa flour
    1 Tbs brown sugar
    1 tsp baking powder
    1/2 tsp baking soda
    1/2 tsp salt
    2 eggs
    1/4 cup melted butter
    butter for greasing the griddle

If you can't find quinoa flour, you can grind your own in a high speed blender.

If you don't have buttermilk you can make it with regular milk curdled with vinegar.

Mix dry ingredients together. Mix wet ingredients together. Combine the two. Do not over-mix (lumps are OK). The batter should be thick, but not too thick. Adjust with extra milk. Spoon mixture onto hot greased griddle or cast iron skillet. The amount you use depends on the size of pancake you want. Turn when holes appear. Cook until golden brown on both sides.

Experiment with varying the amounts of quinoa and whole-wheat flours, or try adding other flours, like buckwheat.

Drop some blueberries into the wet batter before turning for blueberry pancakes.

In my family we always serve pancakes in a stack with sour cream in-between the layers and maple syrup poured over the top.

Quinoa pancakes is one of my very favorite recipes. Quinoa is a perfect ingredient for pancakes, as the hallmark for a great pancake is lightness. Quinoa, being the lightest of all grains, makes the lightest pancakes.

Quinoa pancakes

VI. Photo Credits

The author has made every possible effort to research and credit the sources for all photos. Those not credited below are the property of Stephen Gorad.

Chapter 1
pg. 2   Sergio Larrain
pg. 3, bottom   Don McKinley
pg. 4, bottom   unknown
pg. 7   Cristina Terre

Chapter 2
pg. 30   Silvia Hast Newcomb
pg. 39   David Cusack
pg. 52   David Cusack

Chapter 3
pg. 58   Adobe Stock
pg. 63   Sierra Blanca Associates
pg. 64   Sierra Blanca Associates
pg. 79   Julio Torres
pg. 80   Julio Torres

Chapter 4
pg. 90   Adobe Stock

Chapter 6
pg. 119   unknown
pg. 121   unknown

Chapter 8
pg. 146   Stefan Jeremiah

Chapter 9
pg. 173   Don McKinley

Appendices
All photos   Adobe Stock

Made in the USA
Middletown, DE
06 December 2017